LET'S PLAY BALL!

Inside the Perfect Game

William Humber

LESTER
&ORPEN
DENNYS
PUBLISHERS

ROM

A Lester & Orpen Dennys / Royal Ontario Museum Publication

FIRST EDITION

Canadian Cataloguing in Publication Data

Humber, William, 1949-
   Let's play ball

Associated with an exhibition to be held Mar.-Oct. 1989 at the Royal Ontario Museum.
Bibliography: p.
Includes index.
ISBN 0-88619-217-X

1. Baseball. I. Royal Ontario Museum. II. Title.

GV867.H85 1989   796.357   C89-093052-X

Project and editorial management by Paula Chabanais & Associates
Interior design by Lightfoot Design for Paula Chabanais & Associates
Cover art by Boyko
Jacket design by David Montle

Printed and bound in Canada

Key of Front Cover Illustration
1.   Pam Postema, female umpire, 1980s
2.   Mary Baker, All American Girls Professional Baseball League, 1940s
3.   Jackie Robinson, 1940s & '50s
4.   Joe DiMaggio, 1940s
5.   Ted Williams, 1940s & '50s
6.   Sadaharu Oh, Japan League, 1960s–80s
7.   Babe Ruth, 1910s–30s
8.   Harry Wright, 19th century player/promoter/manager
9.   Alexander Cartwright, creator of modern baseball rules, 1840s
10.   Hank Aaron, 1950s–70s
11.   Cool Papa Bell, 1930s & '40s
12.   William Hulbert, first National Baseball League president, 1876

CONTENTS

FOREWORD

The Royal Ontario Museum is pleased to be associated with Lester & Orpen Dennys in the publication of William Humber's fascinating book on baseball, *Let's Play Ball!* Mr. Humber is the curatorial assistant of the exhibition of the same name, which opens at the Royal Ontario Museum on March 1 and runs until September 4. The exhibition contains many of the most interesting artifacts from the National Baseball Hall of Fame at Cooperstown, New York, along with other items from major private collectors for whose support we are most grateful. All of us at the ROM are confident that the exhibition will be a great success.

The exhibition and this book are also part of the ROM's developing policy of inquiry into contemporary culture and history. This does not mean that we are deserting our historic role of studying the "arts of Man through all the ages": we are merely reassessing our examination of their contemporary results.

We are deeply appreciative of John Labbatt Limited and the Toronto Blue Jays for their sponsorship of the exhibition. The exhibition has reached its high degree of excellence because of the generous support and advice of Howard Talbot, the Director of the Baseball Hall of Fame, and his staff.

Our arrangement with our co-publishers provides that half of the proceeds of *Let's Play Ball!* will go to ROM Enterprises, whose sole purpose is to assist and finance the objectives of the museum.

Eddie Goodman
Chairman
Board of Trustees
Royal Ontario Museum

PREFACE

When the injured Kirk Gibson hit the winning home run in the first game of the 1988 World Series, he forced chroniclers to search for new ways to describe how baseball elevates the commonplace into something magical. The normal events of a game are real—the ball is caught or dropped; the batter strikes out or hits a base or home run; the runner is out or moves from first to home—but the meaning of the game cannot be explained in terms of cause-and-effect or the law of averages. And when something happens on the field that is magical to a fan, other terms of reference must be found.

Commentators like to refer to Bobby Thomson's historic home run in the 1951 playoff game between the Dodgers and the Giants as "the miracle of Coogan's Bluff". Moe Berg, a journeyman major-league catcher, was asked to describe the joys of ballplaying and replied: "It's my theater." To writer Roger Angell, the game fans play in their minds while they are watching the field is enacted on some "interior stadium" where anything is possible.

Even these other terms of reference don't perhaps help to explain why one of North America's major cultural institutions, the Royal Ontario Museum, in Toronto, has chosen to showcase basesball, except insofar as the rich heritage of everyday events has as much meaning and significance to North America as the cultural properties of older civilizations, such as China and the Holy Land.

Baseball represents grand public theatre in the twentieth century, to North America, parts of the Far East, the Caribbean, and Europe. In a time when special-interest groups and diverse cultures have deservedly won a voice world-wide, baseball offers a forum for unanimity.

But, one might ask, isn't baseball just a game? I think not. Its rich and varied history takes it out of time, and its international roots, out of space; it enables generations to meet and factions to merge; ultimately, can something that has entered our private lives to such a degree—infusing our language and our understanding of what is essentially human about us—be less than an integral part of life?

This book is neither a history of the major-league game nor an analysis of the statistics that have accrued around it, although both subjects are explored here. Rather, it is one person's attempt to peel back the layers of this most perfect of games to expose the secret of its charm and the appeal it holds for so many.

Every fan has a favourite memory of the game. Mine is of the Sunday afternoon match on September 8, 1957 (the day before my eighth birthday), held in Toronto's Maple Leaf Stadium between the Triple-A Leafs and Rochester; Toronto took it 4–3, to win the International League pennant by a half game over Buffalo. Archie Wilson's and Mike Goliat's eighth-inning home runs provided the margin, but what I will always remember is the wind that seemed to sweep the park as Rochester's Cot Deal grounded out to end the game, a wind that drove 13,562 fans to their feet to cheer.

One could wait a lifetime for another epiphany so sweet.

ACKNOWLEDGMENTS

Many people assisted in making this book possible: special thanks is owed to Neil Luxton of the Sports Administration program at Durham College for his research and production assistance. I would also like to thank my publishers, Lester & Orpen Dennys and the Royal Ontario Museum, for allowing me to tell stories about baseball. I note in particular the encouragement of Malcolm Lester and Judi Levita at Lester & Orpen Dennys and of my colleagues on the Royal Ontario Museum team responsible for mounting the 1989 exhibition "Let's Play Ball!": John Vollmer, Gwendolyn Smith, Beverly Dywan, Chris Sasaki, Eric Siegrist, and Susan Haight. I would also like to acknowledge the support of my colleagues at Seneca College and, in particular, to thank Tony Tilly and Eleanor Sutton. The Seneca College baseball class and the annual Cooperstown tours led by good friend and fellow baseball crank David Crichton are without equal— my special thanks to Randy Echlin, Harvey Trivett, and Gord Kirke.

Special mention should be made of the helpful staff at many fine libraries, in particular the Newcastle Public Library in Bowmanville, Ontario, and the National Baseball Library in Cooperstown, New York.

Thanks is due also, and in no small measure, to the Society of American Baseball Research, membership in which I treasure.

I would like to thank my international correspondents for their continuing interest in baseball matters, among them Jan Bagin of the Czechoslovakian national baseball team, Henry Tensen in Sierra Leone whose baseball-card collection triggered many fine memories, and SABR members Joe Overfield, Mark Rucker, and Tom Heitz in the United States.

My personal thanks to the Westlakes for their generous provision of a retreat at Orr Lake for research and writing; and to Cathie, my wife; Bradley, Darryl, and Karen, our children; and our many friends in Bowmanville for their assistance.

W.H.
1989

INNING 1

THE GREAT DISCOVERY

Baseball fans were known throughout the nineteenth century as "cranks", a term that reflected not only an interest in things mechanical but also a lack of patience, in an emerging industrial era, with games such as cricket that took several days to play. Baseball, unlike its English cousin, was a game of action, and its followers were soon suggesting that it was the supreme metaphor for the New World.

In the nineteenth century, baseball was a great discovery. The idea that one could look in a newspaper to find out where one's city stood in relation to another by noting the successes of the local ball team was a landmark in the growth of civic pride. For though baseball has roots in folk traditions and rural settings, its modern form is a strictly urban invention. While Al Spalding would try to convince the nation that Abner Doubleday had invented the game in the small New York village of Cooperstown, what Spalding cited as proof was not the birth of baseball but its last stages of rural ascendancy before it was taken over by urban trends.

Baseball gave shared meaning to urban life in cities of strangers. It demonstrated the importance of rules to modern urban industrial society where the diversity of custom and belief meant that life could no longer be a matter of improvisation. It provided a diversion from the rigorous demands of industrialization, offering city dwellers a controlled and understandable forum for the appreciation of human skill. For a people without a common history, it created one and added to it daily. By 1856, William Trotter Porter was calling baseball "our National Game" in New York's *Spirit of the Times*, even though cricket coverage still outnumbered baseball coverage ten to one. Baseball fashioned a sense of place, bringing strangers together in the shared activity of cheering for their home team; at the same time, paradoxically, it created regional and even national identities around common sets of rules and expectations.

Conformity was a cherished goal. In May 1876, Harry Gorman, manager of the London Tecumsehs, on discovering that Canadian rules differed somewhat from American ones, primarily in the calling of balls and strikes, asked his fellow managers, "What shall I do? Keep it every second ball or follow the amended rule of every third? For my own part, I think it would prevent confusion if the regular professional rules are followed." Canadian officials changed the rules to match those of the American game and the last differences between them disappeared.

Opposite: Albert Spalding's baseball-playing tourists on the Sphinx in 1889.

Baseball created new classes of public personalities. As often as not, ballplayers were a rough lot. Chief Meyers of the New York Giants recalled that players were often denied admittance to the better hotels: "Like the sailors in Boston, on the Commons—'No sailors allowed'. We were in that class. We were just second class citizens, even worse."

Newspapers titillated the public with tales of ballplayers' indiscretions. *The Sporting Life* of September 26, 1888, reported: "Ryan, Sullivan and Daly of the Chicago Base Ball Team were brought before Police Justice Woodman yesterday to settle the question whether they ever flirted with anybody in the house of Mrs. Seth Blood.... One of her neighbors, a Pinkerton detective named Kelly, says that it is not a respectable place, because the base ball players on the grounds flirt their handkerchiefs at Mrs. Blood and others in the house, and Mrs. Blood and the others flirt back."

A mid-nineteenth-century baseball game at the Elysian Fields in Hoboken, New Jersey.

However, it was not just the players who were rough and tumble. After Toronto played in Syracuse in September 1888, the team loudly proclaimed its displeasure, in *The Sporting Life*, at the local fans' behaviour:

> Never was such a boisterous and disorderly scene witnessed within a base ball enclosure in Syracuse; that there was one mighty howl throughout the nine innings; that the offensively partisan crowd would not allow the Torontos to run under any circumstances and several times threatened to mob them; that the cyclone gang on the bleaching boards, who blew the paint off their tin trumpets (the Syracuse management supplied about 200 boys and fish horns) were a mighty force in the general din and disorder; that every ruling against the Torontos was cheered to the echo....

No matter the size of a town, it had to have a baseball team. The game burrowed its way into the lifestyle, language, and common experience of people, which does much to explain the enduring fascination it holds and the almost religious status it is accorded now, in our own time of affluence and cultural diversity. The arrival of the bats in a small southwestern Ontario town in the 1880s was a grand event. Lucan, Ontario, had its own team, the Irish Nine, by the 1860s, and twenty years later the game earned a mention in the trial following the massacre of the Black Donnellys in Lucan. "I never played baseball," Bob Donnelly was reported to have said, perhaps in reference to one of the wooden clubs that had been found at the murder site.

As the game matured into the age of technology, it used the new resources of the time to spread its message. The National Association of Base Ball

Players, formed in 1851, owed its genesis to the train that connected the east and midwest. By 1860, the Excelsior Club of Brooklyn rode the rails on its tour through Upper New York State. For most of the next hundred years, rail was the method of transportation, giving the game a more leisurely quality as players cemented friendships during long card games in the carriages, and managers such as Connie Mack could instruct rookies in game fundamentals in a private car. As late as the 1940s, Carl Furillo recalled the run from Chicago to St. Louis: "It was always a beautiful run. I used to love that run. You could sit in the coach and see farm country and wide open spaces."

Newspapers and sporting journals, such as *The Clipper*, relying on the telegraph and later the telephone, found an eager audience for boxscores and detailed game reports.

On the field, the game changed to reflect the emerging skills of the players and demands of the fans. By the early twentieth century, fans could knowledgeably dissect the strategies of different batters—Rogers Hornsby, for instance, who stood in the far rear corner of the box and hit to all fields well; Ty Cobb, who adjusted his position according to the pitcher, standing at the back for a curveballer and waiting for the ball to break, and at the front for a spitballer, hitting the ball before it broke down.

"The Arrival of the Bats"—a street scene in Southern Ontario, 1884.

One hundred years ago, a troop of baseball pioneers set out to spread that

understanding and to preach baseball's gospel to the world. While they largely failed in that enterprise, the story of their quest has become part of a national mythology and is as good a place as any to explore the hidden dreams of baseball.

"There had been noteworthy tours in the history of modern athletes," Henry Palmer of *The New York Herald* said in 1889, "however, the natural game of the Americans had never been carried beyond its shores excepting the 1874 English tour." That lack was corrected in the fall of 1888, when Al Spalding decided to take two ball teams around the world. What resulted was a six-month journey that is unparalleled in sports history, both in its unrestricted gall and in its imaginative leap of faith. The world was still a marvellously fresh and varied place in 1888. Adventurers, entertainers, cyclists, and rowers regularly undertook the hazards of the round-the-world tour, and their tales excited an American population somewhat removed from its frontier past and looking for new challenges. Most importantly for baseball, these stories moved Albert Spalding.

Born in a small Illinois farming village in 1850, Albert Spalding first reached public attention in 1867 when he led the provincial Rockford Forest City club to a sensational 29–23 upset over the acclaimed Washington Nationals. Spalding won 207 games and lost only 56 as a member of Boston's National Association team from 1871 to 1875 and after that won 47 for Chicago in the National League's first season. Within two years, however, he had left the game and was well established as a producer of

The Atlantic Club of Brooklyn versus the Mutual Club of New York, in a championship match at Hoboken, New Jersey, on August 3, 1865.

annual baseball guide books and retailer of sporting goods. Spalding was driven not only by an affinity for private enterprise but also by a peculiar nineteenth-century public spiritedness, which in later years would see him make an unsuccessful run for public office and embrace theosophy. The famous photograph that shows the American baseball party standing on various levels of the Sphinx (opposite page 1) is in some ways a portrait of Spalding's new-world sensibility accommodating an older one.

But the Sphinx was not yet on the agenda on the evening of October 20, 1888, at Chicago's Union Depot, where two magnificently equipped railway coaches awaited Chicago's National League team and the All-Americans, a collection of league players. The players' destination was Australia; later Spalding would reveal his plans to continue around the globe.

Spalding's baseball tourists fêted in Honolulu at the beginning of the World Tour in the fall of 1888.

The travelling party was mixed and included not only players, such as future Hall of Famers Cap Anson and John Montgomery Ward (who joined the tour in Denver); reporters, such as Harry Palmer; invited guests, such as former ballplayer and cricketer George Wright and Spalding's assistant, Harry Simpson, of the Newark club, who would remain in Australia to spread word of the game; but also in an era before the airplane, a skydiver, Professor Bartholomew, who, according to *The Sporting Life*, ascended in a balloon "until he became a speck against the blue sky and then suddenly leaped from his perch out into space, clutching the bar of his parachute which trailed after his rapidly descending figure until the air caught its folds and spread it out like a big umbrella behind him." He had managed to break most of the bones in his body and lost an eye once when he landed in a tree.

The party's mascot was a young black man, Clarence Duval, who had been the attendant to a touring French actress until he was abandoned in Omaha. Dressed in drum major's uniform and twirling a baton, he led the teams onto the field. The American humorist Frank Lincoln also travelled with the team as far as Australia.

A crowd of more than thirteen thousand turned out at the Haight Street grounds to watch the team play in San Francisco, though some of the players, such as John Ward, excused themselves for a day's quail shooting and others toured the city's Chinese quarter, peeking "into foul smelling lodging houses, into opium joints thick with sickening vapours, down through underground passageways, where it would be death for a white man to go alone, into Joss houses, with their hideous idols, their burning tapers and their weird-sounding drums and tomtoms...."

The 2,100-mile boat trip to Honolulu took a week. As only a day was allowed for the stopover and it was a Sunday, the planned ball game was not played, though King Kalakuau did provide a grand banquet at which Frank Lincoln told jokes and Clarence Duval demonstrated several styles of the demeaning plantation dances of the period.

On board ship to Australia, George Wright rigged up a protective netting for one-wicket cricket in expectation that the players would play some games on tour, and it proved to be good exercise. At last the *Alameda* reached New Zealand. A procession of carriages greeted the teams in uniform and the cricket pitch to which they were taken to play ball amazed Palmer: "The way in which a ball rolled whenever it was batted into the smooth, velvety outfield would have broken the hearts of league outfielders in a championship game."

In Australia a few days later, the reception was equally remarkable, and

Poster advertising Spalding's baseball tour to Australia, 1888.

at one gathering, Canadian oarsman Ned Hanlan was introduced as a model to the Americans of the sporting links that could be forged between countries.

The cricket grounds on which they played were superior to anything they had seen in the United States. At one of these grounds, in Melbourne, they met an old colonist and former American, Mr. S.P. Lord, who claimed to have introduced baseball to Australia on his arrival there in 1853.

On Christmas Eve, in 90-degree weather, the batters excited a crowd of six thousand and the game was followed by the performance of a baseball farce, written in the team's honour, at the St. George's Theatre.

The next day, they departed for Adelaide, where they visited the vineyards of Thomas Hardy; descending into his cool vaults, they drank glass after glass before departing for Henley Beach and "spent half an hour

Spalding's World Tour of 1888–89 concluded with matches in Great Britain.

picking up the delicate shells from the wave washed sand, in quaffing mugs of ale...and looking out over the grand old ocean." That afternoon's game was marked by daring base running and magnificent sliding.

On New Year's Day, 1889, only two thousand attended their demonstration, the majority of the holiday crowd favouring football games, played according to Victorian rules, and horse racing.

The *Salier* sailed from Port Melbourne on the morning of January 8 with a passenger load of ballplayers and an emigrant population of Chinese, Sinhalese, Hindus, and Europeans, all bound for the Indian subcontinent. Time would prevent the baseball party from carrying on to India, but they did stop in Ceylon and played possibly the first game ever seen in Colombo. Here they were met by peddlers and beggars crying "baksheesh" and "very hungry", and what a sight the players must have been in full uniform riding to the cricket ground in bullock carts and jinrickshaws. "There were hundreds of howling, chattering, grotesquely arrayed natives with their red, white, green, blue and orange turbans, sashes and jackets," Palmer complained. "It was laughable to see their desperate efforts to get out of the way when a ball was thrown or batted among them."

The party's next stop was the Suez and here they were greeted by donkey boys, who transported them to the train for the trip to Cairo. Again, the novelty overwhelmed the tourists: "on every hand were booths, cafés and places of amusement without number, from roulette wheels, publicly operated, to French opera and inviting brasseries where one can drop in for a puff at a narghili, or for a cup of chocolate and a cigarette served by waitresses of almost any nationality in Asia or Europe."

Camels were provided on February 9 for the All-Americans and donkeys for the Chicago players so that they might visit the Sphinx and the Pyramids and play the first professional ball game ever on Egyptian soil. In the shifting sand at the base of the pyramid of Cheops, they played a five-inning, error-filled game won 10–6 by the All-Americans. Play was occasionally suspended as the players fought with the local Bedouins for possession of the ball. Afterwards, according to Palmer, "after supplying the heathens with backsheesh [sic], the ballplayers prepared to vacate the premises. Before going, every man took a shy at the right eye of the Sphynx [sic] with the ball. Jim Fogarty was the only man who succeeded in giving the colossus a black eye."

A week later, the party arrived in Italy but Spalding's offer of $5,000 and donation of gate receipts to charity failed to sway archaeologists and Italian officials into renting him the Colosseum for a game. Instead, they played before the king and his court at the Villa Borghese.

Europe was a revelation to the ballplayers. They visited the gaming tables of Monte Carlo where coffee was one dollar a cup, they joined the Cancan dancers in Paris, and walked the Rue Montmartre, "a blaze of electric light, brilliant costumes, and vivacious women." Playing in a park on the banks of the Seine within the shadow of the Eiffel Tower, they entertained a crowd of surprised American tourists. In this game, however, Ed Williamson tore up his knee on a sharp stone while sliding into second. He would play only forty-seven games in the coming season and a final seventy-three in 1890 when his career ended, four years before his death at the age of thirty-six.

After a perilous crossing of the English channel in which several of the players were thrown out of their bunks, the team prepared for the largest receptions of the entire tour. It was now late March, fog and rain shrouded London, and the ground was soft, black, and sticky. Still, with the Prince of Wales in attendance at the Kennington Oval, along with the great man of English cricket, Dr. W.G. Grace, there was no question that a game would be played. Though he described baseball as an excellent sport, the prince told Spalding that he still considered cricket superior.

The team was later introduced in the House of Commons, where Sir William Harcourt was speaking on "The Treatment of Political Prisoners in Ireland". Games followed at the venerable Lords cricket ground and in other locations throughout England, though spectators were more amused by the American pitchers trying to strike out English cricketers in post-game exhibitions or longest-throw contests between the ballplayers and their cricket-playing hosts.

The players were provided with a special nine-car train with the inscription "The American Baseball Clubs" on the side for the tour of Birmingham, Sheffield, Bradford, and Manchester, as well as Scotland.

The game of rounders arranged between an American eleven and the Rounders Association of Liverpool was perhaps the most curious match of the tour. Rounders had been a primary influence on early forms of baseball in America, but in England it was largely children's play, except in Liverpool and South Wales where adults had taken it up. The fielders were positioned much like in baseball except for an additional player behind the catcher and an additional fielder. The bat was swung with one hand, three-foot iron stakes served as bases, the runner was retired by having the ball thrown at him, and, as in early baseball, pitching was straight-armed. Rounders as played in Liverpool was an evolution from the same fossil from which American baseball sprung, but according to Palmer, "This was all we saw of the Rounders during our tour of the world, and I am quite certain neither of our party cared to see any more of it." Liverpool won the two-inning game 16 to14.

For Tom Daly, Jim Manning, John Tener, and others, the highlight of the trip was the return to their ancestral land of Ireland. When Manning reached his uncle's home in Callan in Kilkenny, he was greeted by a display of clippings about his baseball career pinned to the wall. "Of course I had a delightful time," he recalled, "and everything in Callan, even the scores of pretty Irish girls, was mine."

The voyage home was uneventful though marked by turbulent seas and a sighting of the *Adriatic* off New York's Fire Island early Saturday morning, April 6, 1889. But still the tour was not allowed to finish. An exhibition game was held in Brooklyn two days later and that evening, one of the grandest dinners of nineteenth-century America was held at Delmonico's, presided over by the baseball establishment. It was here that Mark Twain, as guest speaker, described the game as "the very symbol,

Opening game at the Polo Grounds, 1886, between New York and Boston.

*Vendor at South Side Ball Park,
Chicago, in 1905.*

the outward and visible expression for the drive and push and rush and struggle of the raging, tearing, booming, nineteenth century."

Of their trip to Hawaii, Twain said that it had been akin to "interrupting a funeral with a circus.... Baseball is all fact, the Islands all sentiment." Following response to the toasts, DeWolf Hopper portrayed in verse the troubles of the New York club in holding on to their Polo Grounds ball-park on 111th Street.

Games and more dinners followed. At one dinner, Spalding predicted great things for the game in New Zealand and Australia, little possibility in Ceylon, Egypt, and Italy; in Arabia, he said, "there is no more chance for the game than for a blacklisted player to enter Heaven." Of the English, he was more positive, though he believed their innate conservatism would be a hindrance.

Montgomery Ward, on behalf of his teammates, said simply, "There is no period in my professional life that I will look back to with more genu-ine pleasure than upon the six months past." Another speaker, in reply to all the testimonials, promised, "When the national game is carried out to the extent Mr. Spalding has predicted, when we have the international game, you will say, 'I was one of the band who went around the world and showed the world what the national game was capable of.' "

Returning at last to Chicago, 32,000 miles after their departure, the remnants of the touring group were met by a huge crowd, music, calcium lights, coloured torches and rockets, and Roman candles bursting over their heads. At one last dinner, Cap Anson noted that the attendance of the English prince had raised "the social standard of the national game to the highest point it had yet attained."

Viewed in retrospect, the world tour had little impact on ballplaying habits around the world, but in America, its conception and realization had been a marvellous, imaginative success. In taking the game to the world, Spalding brought to America an enduring national symbol.

By the end of the nineteenth century journalists were beginning to use "baseball" to refer to the game, abandoning the century-long tradition of the two-word version ("base ball"), which in the minds of its players and fans told much about the game's origins. The story of where the base and the ball came from is a journey to a distant past.

INNING 2

INVENTING BASEBALL

Baseball began as magic. While the game as we know it was not played until the mid-nineteenth century, versions of it appeared in art and literature in earlier times, sometimes in primitive or highly advanced forms. The Norse played *cat* as part of a ritual celebration of the arrival of the late northern spring planting season. In southern India, a Dravidian hill tribe played a bat and ball game called *pulat*; in the Yucatan, a predecessor of the game formed part of the ceremonies conducted in the ball court of the Temple of Warriors; the Russian folk game *lapta* is very similar to English rounders; and, in Egypt, the tomb of Beni Hassan shows a ball game in progress.

In 1906 Albert Spalding, the sporting-goods entrepreneur, struck a blue-ribbon commission of seven baseball authorities to investigate the game's origin. By 1908, to his undoubted satisfaction (some suggest, to his specification), the commission concluded that while simple versions of the game had existed prior to 1839, baseball itself was the product of Abner Doubleday's genius in laying out the diamond and the rules that year in Cooperstown, New York. The commission's report (its notes, affidavits, and various corroborating documents were lost in a fire) relies heavily on a letter from an elderly Denver resident, Abner Graves, who remembered learning the game from Doubleday in 1839. We have since discovered that Doubleday was unlikely to have been anywhere near Cooperstown that year and that the rules that supposedly emerged from his genius were almost identical to those of English rounders, described in *The Boy's Own Book*, published in London in 1828.

A trip to the local sandlot would have brought Spalding's commission closer to the origins of the game. In almost any open space where children gather, some form of baseball, its rules dictated by circumstance but its ideas the time-honoured ones of the game's tradition, will be in play. Tag and street stickball, fragments of an ancient form of baseball, don't need to be learned but are part of a universal folk memory of play.

Wilson Green, a Manitoba historian, recalled a game played in a concession backlot around the turn of the century:

It was a rough, primitive game we played occasionally as small (and not so small) boys, requiring only sticks or clubs and something in the shape of a ball, sometimes even a frozen horse dropping (as in road hockey). All but one player (no set number; say, under eight) dug a hollow depression in which he kept his "bat" until getting a swipe at the dead or rolling ball in any direc-

Opposite: By the late nineteenth century, the organized-playground movement was providing adult direction to children's spontaneous play, which in time led to organized little-league baseball. Retaining their independent spirit, twentieth-century inner-city children created the street game stickball in which fire hydrants, car bumpers, and manhole covers serve as bases.

tion. While one was doing this, another could slip his stick into the vacated base. In this way, the odd player could occupy any vacant hole he found. The game got underway by one lad heaving the bundle of bats as far as possible, excepting his own. The player who was unable to return to his (or any) depression was required to keep the ball in play until finding an opening himself. The game invariably ended in one or more fights. It was based on skullduggery, not sportsmanship.

What distinguishes games of this type is spontaneity, creativity, and informality—the features of baseball before its rigorous codification in the nineteenth century.

How far back baseball's forebears can be traced is perhaps anyone's guess. Complex forms of the game appear at certain points in history, only to be followed by simplified corruptions. It is as though the trail left by the game's antecedents had been marked by someone determined to confound all pursuers.

A 1937 expedition to Libya, led by Italian anthropologist Corrado Gini, to investigate a strain of blondness among Berber tribes, found tribesmen in the village of Jadum playing what could only be described as a rudimentary form of baseball. Gini eventually concluded that these blond Berbers were probably descended from northern colonists who had come to North Africa some six thousand to three thousand years before Christ. The tribesmen's game, *Ta kurt om el mahag* ("ball of the mother of the pilgrim"), was played only in this region of North Africa, an area untouched by influences from other cultures. The playing field was a level space with a home base located near a shady area and a running base (*el mahag*) some seventy to ninety feet away. The ninety-foot distance aside, Corrado Gini's description of the game leaves little doubt as to its similarity to baseball:

> The batting team strikes the [leather-covered] ball in batting order with a bat, sending it as far off as possible, so that the other members of the team may have time to run from home to the *mahag*, and if possible, back again. The men of the fielding team try to prevent this by catching the ball as it flies, or picking it up from the ground and throwing it to a member of the batting team, as he runs from the gate to the *mahag*, or back. When a team bats, it is called "marksmen" (*darraba*), and when it fields, it is called "hunters" (*fajadah*).

In the Berber game, the intent of the pitcher is to let the batter make contact with the ball, a notion that persisted in the modern form of the game until 1887, when the batter's right to call for a specified type of pitch was finally rescinded. A Berber batter who made two strikes (three, for the captain) was retired and said to be "rotten" or to "grow mouldy", terms that strongly suggest that the game was part of a ritualized plea for rain. Even though the Berbers themselves took the pragmatic view that the game was merely a form of exercise that built a warrior's muscle and improved his wind capacity, they believed that in the long run it ensured that the year would be prosperous. Their denial of the game's magical purpose notwithstanding, the tribesmen understood that prosperity in North Africa was linked to rain.

The similarities of the Berber game to ones played by an older culture indicate that blondness was not the sole legacy that the Norse colonizers left in Jadum.

Longball, played as part of a springtime or Easter festival in the Middle Ages in Scandinavia, is markedly like *Ta kurt om el mahag*. In longball, the

Unknown player, c. 1868.

"out" players or fielders were called "rotten" and the "in" players or batters, "fresh"—a distinction that carries associations of winter and spring.

A regional variation of longball, "Northern Spell" (from the Old Norse *knur*, referring to a small knot of wood, and *spil*, meaning "game") is indistinguishable from the English game *cat* (an Old English word that is synonymous with *knur*). In *cat*, which has a place in English literature in such diverse works as Bunyan's *The Pilgrim's Progress* and Dickens's *Pickwick Papers*, a ball-like piece of wood with conical ends was flipped into the air and hit with a stick to waiting fielders. In the various forms of the game, once the ball was hit, the runners moved from one hole to another, hoping to reach the next before the *cat* was tossed between two bases.

Trapball, a form of *cat* played in the north of England, used a spring device to pitch the ball up into hitting range and involved the notions of three-strike outs and being caught out on a fly ball. Stoolball, a simplified form of trapball, had the batter trying to bat away a pitch aimed at a stool behind him. Originally played as part of Easter celebrations, stoolball eventually became one-wicket cricket, the prototype of the game that flourished on the wide lawns of the south of England in the eighteenth century.

As the Scandinavian forms of the game filtered down from the north, other European versions appeared from the continent. A German game, described in 1796, had the pitcher toss the ball in a gentle arc to the batter,

New York Metropolitans of the American Association, 1886, at St. George's Cricket Field on Staten Island, New York.

Early baseball scene c. 1850s. Note the pitcher's under-arm delivery and catcher's distance from home plate.

first base, then second, then back to the hitting goal. This game was similar in many ways to the medieval French *theque* or *tec* and *balle empoisonée*, games with four to six bases, in which the batter is allowed three strikes at the ball; if he hits three for the "ronde" (three circuits of the bases) his team remains at bat.

The word *ronde* and the games associated with it came to England from France, met the Scandinavian traditions of such games as "Northern Spell", and eventually became "rounders". Played on a diamond with a base at each corner, rounders required a "feeder" to toss the ball in an arc to a batter, who was allowed three refusals. Missing three or a ball caught on the fly constituted an out and running the bases after a successful hit scored a run for each base touched. The game, no longer a rite of spring and supplanted by cricket as a favoured adult bat-and-ball game, was turned over to the children.

The French roots of baseball extend not only from medieval "poisoned ball" but also from the old English game of base running or *barres*. As long ago as the reign of Edward III in the fourteenth century, English children played a game in which they ran from one bar or base to another, sometimes without the element of bat and ball. The sport of base running, mentioned by Spenser in *The Faerie Queen* ("So ran they all as they had been at base, / they being chased that did others chase") and by Shakespeare in *Cymbeline* ("He, with two striplings—lads more like to run / The country base than to commit such slaughter"), was eventually banned in the avenues leading to Westminster Palace by Parliament.

As early as 1744 an English book describing twenty-six diversions for children listed "base ball" under "B". Four years later, Lady Harvey's letters included this notation: "The Prince of Wales and his family divert themselves at base ball, a game all schoolboys are acquainted with." Just how diverting such games could be was remarked upon by Jane Austen in

Northanger Abbey (written in 1798–99): "[I]t was not very wonderful that Catherine…should prefer cricket [and] base ball…to books."

Baseball came to America with immigrants from the southeastern counties of England (apparently they left behind the word "rounders"; Moor's *Suffolk Words* lists only "base ball"). George Ewing (1754–1824) records in his journals in 1778:

> April 7
> Exersised [*sic*] in the afternoon in the intervals played at base this evening some Rogueish chaps tied a sheaf of straw to the tail of Josephs Andersons Bquartermaster commonly called leg and a piece of five Pound tens horse tail and set it on fire and let him run which very much offended him and he set out to the Genl to enter a complaint…

"Baste-ball" was being played at Princeton around this time, and Thurlow Weed, a Rochester politician and newspaper editor, made a note in his memoirs of "a base ball club organized about 1825" (the one-word form "baseball" did not have wide currency in America until the end of the nineteenth century). Americans took what they knew of rounders and an older Dutch bat-and-ball game and came up with "townball". Three, four, or five bases were marked with stones on central village greens on the day of the annual town meeting. Players were as numerous as those eager to join in, and a runner was out when a flyball was caught or when hit by the ball between bases. One version of townball was eventually codified as the Massachusetts game in the early nineteenth century, the first formal attempt to wrest the game back from the children.

Cricket was an adult preserve in England since the eighteenth century and a sophisticated, virtually professional sport since the nineteenth when it was discovered by aristocratic gamblers and players were hired to play for a fee. It came to America as a mature, codified sport, but failed to incite the same fervour in its new, less aristocratic home. Cricket failed in America, according to historian Mel Adelman, not only because it required more advanced bat-and-ball skills than those possessed by the average American player, but also because the rules of play were strictly defined and intolerant of the kind of experimentation that Americans were eager to use in adapting the game to their own particular circumstances. In the frontier, fertile ground existed for the child's game of rounders to be cultivated into a serious and, eventually, professional sport.

John Chadwick, an Exeter journalist and a member of the Gloucester Rounders Association, emigrated to America in 1772 and helped to sow the seeds of the game's success there.

The first American book on baseball was Robin Carver's *The Book of Sports*, published in 1834, six years after *The Boy's Own Book* , and adopting the rules for rounders printed there as the basis for "base" or "goal" ball. If rounders was still considered child's play by most, baseball was changing.

The special place in baseball history reserved for Alexander Cartwright and his New York Knickerbockers is well documented. Cartwright, at various times a surveyor, bookseller, and Knickerbocker volunteer fire-fighter, published a set of rules for the game of baseball in 1845 from which our fascination with the modern game evolved.

Cartwright's game stipulated that there would be nine men on the field, that the bases would be ninety feet apart, and that "soaking" (throwing the ball at an opposition player to retire him) would be outlawed. Known as "the New York game", Cartwright's version fought for supremacy against other, often more longstanding, regional practices until the 1860s. The outcome of the battle was unpredictable for years.

Historian Lawrence Kart describes two of the earlier competing "games":

> By 1800, two distinct forms had merged. The Massachusetts game had bases 60 feet apart in an open quadrangle with the striker placed halfway between first and home, a "one out, all out" rule (formerly every man had to be put out before the sides changed), a limit of 14 players per team, and a definite conclusion—the first side to score 100 runs was the winner. The Philadelphia game was even closer to modern baseball, with the striker standing at the home base corner of an elongated diamond, a 9 inning rule instead of the 100 run total to conclude play, and a more genteel way of putting the runner out—either he or the base he was headed for could be tagged with the ball.

While Kart's date of 1800 seems rather early, it is fair to conclude that both these competing versions of the game predated Cartwright's. A townball team existed in Philadelphia from 1833 to almost 1860, when the New York game was adopted there, and a Buffalo version (closer to the Massachusetts game) held out until 1857 before the New York rules took precedence.

Reproduction of an early print entitled Union Prisoners at Salisbury, North Carolina. *Ball playing during the Civil War helped spread the game throughout America.*

In the 1850s in southwestern Ontario, another variation struggled for sway. Differing from its closest American competitor, the Ontario version allowed eleven men on the field, adding to Cartwright's nine men a fourth baseman and a backstop behind the catcher, all of whom had to be retired for the other team to come up to bat. Massachusetts allowed ten to fourteen players and only one man had to be retired. However, Ontario allowed the pitcher to throw overhand, in the modern style—something that, unusually, was banned in New York but legal in Boston.

"The Canadian game" remained popular until the end of the decade, as did the policy of playing against members of one's own club but not against players from other teams or towns. On May 24, 1859, the Toronto Young Canadians defeated the Hamilton Young Americans 68 to 41, using

The New York Knickerbockers at play in the Elysian Fields against a New York Nine in 1846.

New York rules, no gloves, little skill, and the rule that the hitter could designate the position of the pitch.

However, it was the Hamilton Burlingtons' loss to the Buffalo Niagaras in 1860, in the first-ever international match, that marked the end of the Canadian game. Buffalo played the New York rules and the pragmatic young merchants and businessmen of the Burlington club (formed in 1855, with fifty members, and playing on Mondays, Wednesdays, and Fridays on the grounds near Upper James and Robinson streets) willingly converted. Others soon followed.

The Hamilton Maple Leafs (formerly the Young Americans) debated the merits of the styles of play. Arthur Feast, a stonemason who was to popularize the game in Guelph, supported Bill Shuttleworth's defence of the Canadian rules, but Charles Wood, a young innkeeper from the United States, won the day with his support for the New York game. In Woodstock, Bill's younger brother, Jim Shuttleworth, helped to organize a team in 1860, playing the game on Reeves Street, behind the post office, and defeating the Rough and Ready club of Ingersoll twice that year. Characteristic of the fraternal nature of the game, the rival teams dined together after the first match at Woodstock's Royal Exchange Hotel. By 1861, however, Charles Wood had convinced the Woodstock players to switch to the New York rules, and the Canadian game was gone for good.

The New York Knickerbockers, besides championing the form of the game that was to be universally adopted in North America, were the first adults to acknowledge their primary allegiance to baseball as opposed to cricket. Many cricket teams played baseball as a warmup activity and brought to it superior bat-and-ball skills characteristic of the more advanced game. In 1846 the Knicks lost their first baseball match to another club of more skilled cricketers by a disputed score of 23 to 1 (the dispute was over whether the Knicks had in fact scored eleven runs, not one). Attention shifted to the warmup activity and led to the birth of the New York game.

There was something about the New York rules (essentially the rules that govern the game today) that appealed to players and spectators alike. Having eliminated "soaking", Cartwright introduced to the play a smaller, cricket-type ball, which could be hit farther and harder, and expanded the dimensions of the game beyond the infield. As well, his rules led to a quicker exchange between offence and defence and, when their adoption became widespread, made it easier to organize matches between clubs. With the expansion of competition, a new style of play emerged to suit the rules, and the easy-going fraternal character of the game disappeared. By the 1850s, large unruly crowds—throwbacks to the fierce fan rivalry that accompanied the townball matches of New England in the past and predecessors of the incomparable New York Yankee fans of today— became part of the game. The Brooklyn Atlantics had their loyal blue-collar supporters, and their rivals, the Excelsiors, appealed to the white-collar merchants and clerks. Debates of the relative merits of rival teams ceased to be gentlemanly as loyalties split along class or occupational lines. Ultimately, it was in saloons, cigar stores, pool halls, and bookmaking establishments that the fervour that surrounds modern baseball emerged.

Gambling on the outcome of games changed the tenor of baseball from entertainment to economics. In time, that shift would lead to the hiring of players to guarantee victory. James Creighton, hired by Brooklyn in the late 1850s, appears to have been among the first professional players. Patronage was often the currency of the sweetheart deal. In New York, the political machinery of Tammany Hall provided jobs for members of the New York Mutuals, and Washington players were given government sinecures in the 1860s.

By the end of the decade, the game's leading newspaper spokesman, Henry Chadwick, acknowledged that, at least at the level of the best players, baseball had become a business. It had also become a kind of advertising agent for newly emerging cities and towns eager to boost their image at home and abroad.

According to historian Ted Vincent, "sportswriters, poolroom keepers and sponsors of rowing regattas and spirit races were hometown boosters with a special purpose—selling community spirit and unity where diverse social groups seemed to be at one another's throats...." The liveliness of this boosterism and the intense competition that fuelled it were sparked by the perceived economic, cultural, and social threat posed by the hated big metropolis, and the boasts of small-town baseball promoters that their players could "knock the stuffing out of the old leaguers" were often taken literally.

In 1869, Aaron Champion, a Cincinnati businessman, hired Harry Wright, a prominent cricketer, to recruit for an entirely professional club that would come to be known as the Red Stockings. Earning salaries ranging from $600 to $1,400, the players toured the nation on the Union Pacific Railroad, making stops in such places as St. Louis, San Francisco, Sacramento, and Omaha and attracting, in total, more than 100,000 spectators, winning fifty-seven games and tying one, with no losses.

Once baseball teams had joined the round of tournaments and tours, it was a short step to the idea of forming a league. The National Association of Professional Base Ball Players was formed in 1871. Erratic scheduling and the elimination of Chicago, the only serious challenger, by the Great Fire of 1871, which destroyed the city's seven-thousand-seat park and its

Harry Wright was a member of America's second famous family of Wright brothers. A player, manager, and organizer of international tours, he was the first to note, in an 1869 letter, a new custom: "The spectators all arise between halves of the seventh, extend their legs and arms, and sometimes walk about."

"Let us get away from the old wornout title 'National Association of Base Ball Players', and call it 'The National League of Professional Base Ball Clubs'," William Hulbert said, and on February 2, 1876, the league that today is dubbed the "senior circuit" came to be.

competitive spirit, meant that the Boston Red Stockings, managed by Harry Wright and featuring such skilled players as his brother George, Ross Barnes, and Al Spalding, too often dominated during the association's five-year history.

While teams were originally run as a kind of players' collective, with local entrepreneurs backing them out of an interest in public service more than significant private gain, the structure of professional baseball began to change in 1876. Chicago entrepreneur William Hulbert signed up the best players from the Red Stockings and, facing the likelihood that his team would be expelled from the National Association, formed his own National League. According to Albert Spalding, Hulbert recognized that "means ought to be adopted to separate the control of the executive management from the players and the playing of the game."

The old notion of the players' collective with entrepreneurial backing survived in the National League's first serious rival, the International Association. In later years considered by many to have been a minor league, the International Association rejected the National League's authority over administrative matters and set about to purchase the best talent available. Its first champion club, the London Tecumsehs, was, in 1877, one of the top three teams in North America and in mid-season defeated the National League's Chicago team during the first attempt at what we now think of as the World Series. London rejected National League membership at season's end because it would limit the Tecumsehs' ability to stage exhibition games with nearby Guelph and Buffalo. It would be ninety years before another Canadian city, Montreal, would be offered a similar opportunity.

While the National League was severely tested by its rivals over the years, including the Player's League, which was founded in 1890 and rejected Hulbert's belief in the division of labour and management, it survived and remains today, especially in its rejection of the designated-hitter rule, more conservative than its counterpart, the American League.

Formed in 1901 after many years of play as a minor league known as the American Association and based largely in the American midwest, the American League announced its rivalry as a major league that same year. Under the aggressive leadership of Ban Johnson, the league invaded National League territory, luring players with offers of higher salaries and the promise that umpires would be given full support in their efforts to curb the rough-and-tumble of the game. By 1903, the American League's membership had stabilized, with teams from Boston, Philadelphia, Cleveland, New York, Detroit, St. Louis, Chicago, and Washington—a roster that held for fifty years, until the St. Louis Browns transferred to Baltimore.

While the end-of-season competition in the 1880s between the National League and the American Association was described by the media as a world series, that event, as we know it, was not staged until 1903, when Cy Young's Boston Pilgrims defeated Honus Wagner's Pittsburgh Pirates five games to three. The event was vetoed by New York Giants' manager, John McGraw in 1904, but the fall classic, or "world serious" in Ring Lardner's phrase, was reinstated in 1905 and thereafter was an annual event.

William Hulbert's idea that the players and the play should be separate from the financial management of the game seems odd today, now that contract gamesmanship in baseball boardrooms is as newsworthy as anything that happens on ballpark diamonds. In 1879, the reserve clause was introduced, securing a player's services in perpetuity and, for almost a century, artificially limiting salaries until, with the introduction of limited free agency in the 1970s, the tight elastic band popped off the bankrolls.

In some ways, money supplanted the magic—organized baseball today seems as far removed from its magical origins as the *Wall Street Journal* is from *The Tibetan Book of the Dead*. Yet, the almost mystical attractions of the game have never been stronger. From spring training to the fall classic, the game still has all the old seasonal connections that inspired its early forms and, insofar as a batter still hits a ball and runs the bases, the game as played by the Bronx Bombers is little removed from that played by the Blond Berbers.

One final note, however, sheds some new light on Abner Doubleday, Spalding's efforts to have him canonized, and the idea of the magic of the game. In a lengthy letter to *Sporting Life* magazine, which appeared in Philadelphia on May 5, 1886, Dr. Adam Ford of Denver, Colorado, described the rules, the players, and the spectators of a game played in Beachville, Ontario, on June 4, 1838. The game witnessed by Ford was baseball in transition from an innocent celebratory game for children to the modern professional sport we know.

That baseball was played in the southwestern Ontario community of Beachville in the 1830s is not surprising: land-hungry Americans, many claiming to be United Empire Loyalists, had settled in the area in the late eighteenth and early nineteenth centuries. That this essentially American pastime was being played a year after the failed Upper Canada Rebellion against American ideas of government seems a little odd, however, especially since a local Beachville wagonmaker was eventually executed for his role in the uprising, but can, perhaps, be explained by the fact that the roots of the game in 1838 were still more clearly European than American. Ford's description shows, in fact, that the Beachville ballplayers were rather modern in their interpretation of the game.

On a smooth pasture behind Enoch Burdick's shops, a company of Scottish Volunteers, still mopping up after the previous year's skirmishing, joined the local spectators to watch Old Ned Dolson and more youthful members of the Burdick, Martin, Karn, Williams, Crittenden, Burtch, and Dodge families play ball, as described by Ford:

The Maple Leaf Base Ball Club of Guelph, Ontario, 1870.

> The infield was a square, the baselines of twenty-one yards long, on which were placed five bags....The distance from the thrower to the catcher was 18 yards....The club (we had bats in cricket but we never used bats in playing base ball) was generally made of the best cedar, blocked with an ax and finished on a shaving horse with a drawing knife....The ball was made of double and twisted woollen yarn...and covered with good honest calf skin, sewed with waxed ends by Edward McNames, a shoemaker....We had fair and unfair balls. A fair ball was one thrown to the knocker at any height between the bend of his knee and the top of his head, near enough to him to be fairly within reach. All others were unfair....When a man struck at a ball it was a strike, and if a man struck at the ball three times and missed it he was out if the ball was caught every time either on the fly or on the first bound.

Twenty-one rounds decided the match, although Ford does talk of innings, and teams had upwards of twelve players a side. In appearance, this 1838 game is very similar to the Massachusetts game or American townball with its roots in English rounders. Ford's description is also very similar to another fond and freely offered remembrance of a game, and the events of Ford's life, as sleuthed out by University of Western Ontario graduate student Nancy Bouchier, make that similarity intriguing.

Dr. Ford left St. Mary's, Ontario, in disgrace, moving to Denver in the early 1880s after a local temperance leader had died mysteriously in his office. Whether Ford told Abner Graves about the Beachville game and

Rain Delay: *Charcoal sketch by Norman Rockwell for the cover of* The Saturday Evening Post, *April 23, 1949.*

Following:

Popularized in the 1880s, fielding gloves as late as the 1920s were still little more than flat pieces of leather with no pocket—hence the term "pancake gloves".

"As he moved, centre stage moved with him"—author Roger Kahn on Babe Ruth.

Willow, hickory, and ash have all been tried, but today, mountain ash is favoured, for its resiliency and strength, in bat production.

In 1952, Baseball *magazine screamed from its cover: "TV Must Go ... or Baseball Will." The game survived but the magazine, like many other popular journals, did not.*

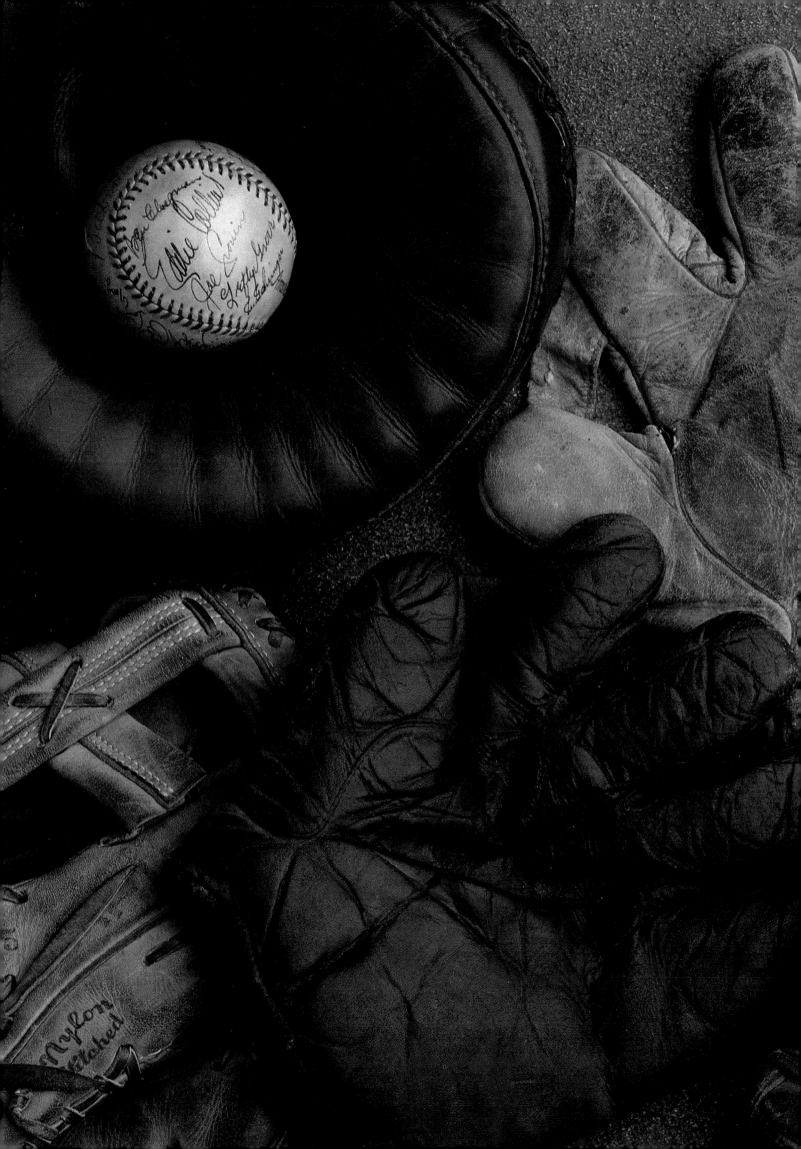

Nineteenth-century sheet music.

whether it was that game, relocated, on which the findings of the Spalding Commission were based must remain a subject of speculation. Dr. Ford, like Abner Doubleday, died before he could comment on the Cooperstown myth. That myth became permanently enshrined in 1939 with the opening of the Baseball Hall of Fame in the small Upper New York State community that cherishes it. Visitors bring the magic of their own memories of childhood sandlot games to Cooperstown and find in the exhibits honouring the game's heroes and achievements the perfect setting in which to contemplate the magic that is baseball. The visitor leaves with the feeling that if baseball was not invented here, it should have been.

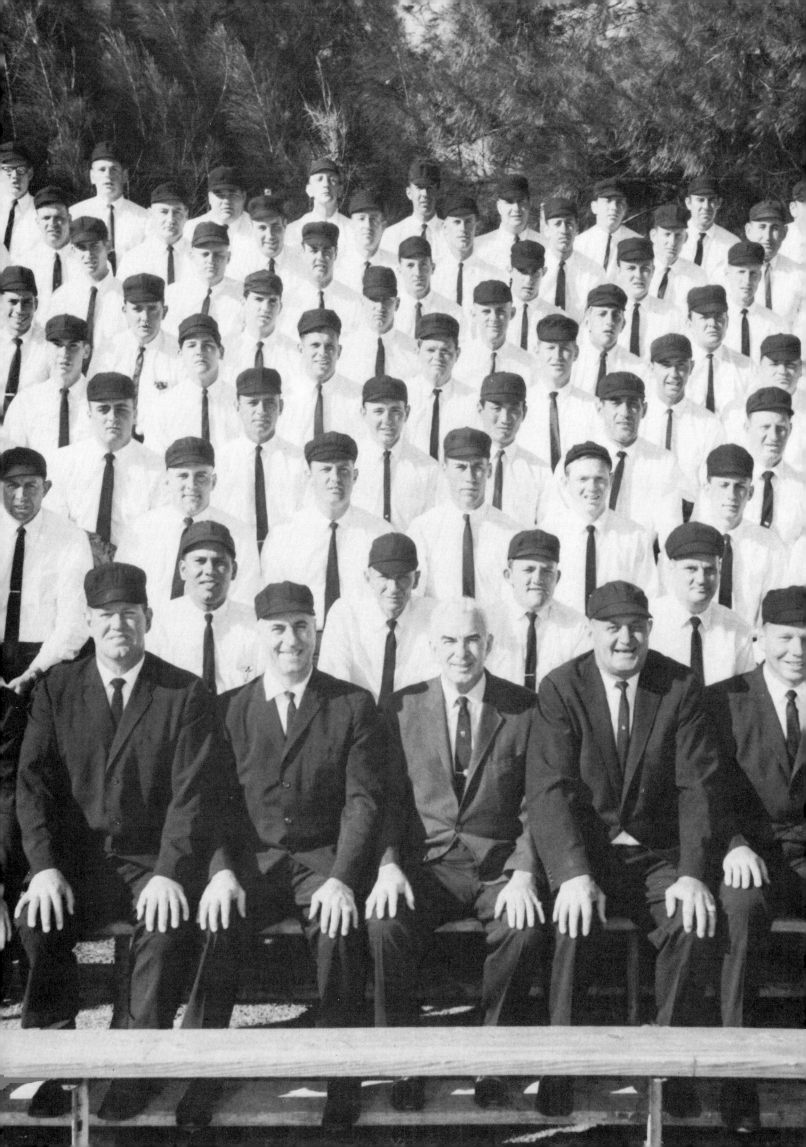

BY THE RULES

There is perhaps nothing as essentially meaningless as a ball game and yet nothing that can so readily inflame passion, bond a crowd of strangers together, and invoke unrestrained glee and blackest despair (just ask a Red Sox fan about the sixth game of the 1986 World Series, when his team was one out away from the title and managed to squander a two-run lead and the subsequent seventh game). And at the centre of this wondrous paradox is the official code of the game—its rulebook. The rules are reinterpreted occasionally to meet the requirements of players' skills and unusual characteristics of individual sandlots, but at their root is the charitable notion of fairness, embodied in the umpires and the requirement that they make the right call. It is for this reason that baseball has the balk and the infield-fly rule, allows for appeals, and unlike any other sport, respects the right of the field manager to seek clarification on the field. And it is why the umpire must at times question intentions—as close as many game officials ever come to weighing men's souls and rendering judgement.

The first rulebook of baseball adopted by the Knickerbocker club on September 23, 1845, contained only twenty guidelines. Of these, the first eight dealt with pre-game matters. Respecting cricket's tradition, it was noted in item two that the "President or, on his absence, the Vice-President, shall appoint an Umpire, who shall keep the game in a book provided for that purpose, and note all violations of the By-Laws and Rules during the time of exercise."

In these early days of the organized game, the umpire had far fewer rules to consult and thus had more power to make arbitrary decisions. However, as in children's games today, the game's folk tradition provided an understood basis for play, and either differences were settled quickly, as befits gentlemen, or everyone went home. The rules referred constantly to exercise rather than competition, suggesting that the game was intended only for play among colleagues. Since the Knickerbockers were the first significant organized club, this is not surprising, and it suggests again that the Knickerbockers must have suffered greatly when their bat-and-ball skills were matched against those of superior cricketers who had consented, perhaps reluctantly, to play baseball.

It was the requirement of this early game that the ball be pitched (not thrown) straight armed and underhand to the bat; that a ball batted outside the range of the first or third base line was foul; that three balls struck at and missed, with the last one caught, was a hand out; that a ball struck, tipped, and caught either flying or on the first bound, was a hand

Opposite: Umpire School Graduating Class, 1967; E.S. Doherty, Jr., Administrator. "Many fans look upon an umpire as a sort of necessary evil to the luxury of baseball, like the odor that follows an automobile" —Pitcher Christy Mathewson in his Pitching in a Pinch (1914).

out; that a player was out if the adversary on the base being approached held the ball or if the runner was touched with it before he made base (and in no instance was a ball to be thrown at him); that a runner who prevented an adversary from catching or getting the ball before he made his base was an out; and that with three outs, all were out. The game consisted of twenty-one counts or aces, but an equal number of hands (the word "innings" was borrowed sometime later from cricket) had to be played. And wouldn't Babe Ruth have shuddered at the final rule that "but one base is allowed when a ball bounds out of the field when struck."

This general set of guidelines was fine when all abiding by them were friends, but within ten years, Cartwright's New York game had a firm hold on the metropolis and was making its way into communities where formerly the Philadelphia game and Massachusetts game had flourished.

The slow demise of the game's fraternal nature brought some features of the 1845 rules into question. Cartwright's regulations suggested that the teams should be as equal as possible, the same standard that a children's pickup game observes today. Inter-club rivalry, however, often resulted in unequal rallies, and the requirement of twenty-one runs for victory could produce some pretty short games. In 1857, the game became a contest spread over nine innings, regardless of the score.

Since, in the 1845 rules, a strike counted only on an unsuccessful swing, there was nothing to prevent the batter from standing at the plate as long as he wished. While the influence of cricket is unmistakable in this, it could hardly satisfy young men who much preferred baseball because it allowed for a quick exchange between offence and defence. And so, in 1858, steps were taken to introduce "called" strikes; and by 1861, the requirement was tightened to read "Should a striker stand at the bat without striking at good balls repeatedly pitched to him for the apparent purpose of delaying the game, or of giving advantage to a player, the umpire after warning him, shall call one strike, and if he persists in such action, two and three strikes. When three strikes are called, he shall be subject to the same rules as if he had struck at three balls." This rule marks a fundamental shift in the game's proportions. Whereas before, the baseball pitcher had been nothing more than a glorified "trap" (the instrument in medieval trapball that projected the ball into the air for the batter to swing at), the instituting of this rule respected the pitcher's independence and allowed him to introduce some of the features of play that are now taken for granted.

While in the interest of fair play it was still expected that the pitcher would toss balls that a hitter could handle, there was, in fact, nothing to prevent him from putting a little extra on the ball, adjusting the speed of a pitch to keep the batter off balance, or aiming at the corners to prompt the batter to swing at a questionable pitch to avoid hearing a strike called.

To assist the batter, therefore, the rules were changed in 1866: "Should the pitcher repeatedly fail to deliver to the striker fair balls, for any cause, the umpire must call one ball; and if the pitcher persists in such action, two or three balls. When three balls shall have been called, the striker shall take first base without being put out...."

The problem with this type of decision-making is that it asks the umpire to measure intent. With his team trailing by one run late in the game, might a batter not ignore a borderline toss in the hope of drawing a base on balls? Might a pitcher not as well try to get the batter to nibble at a questionable pitch and hope the umpire rewards his cleverness by calling a fair pitch?

The first step towards a rigorous definition of a strike zone was an 1871 rule that allowed batters to call for a high ball, low ball, or fair ball (a pitch between the shoulder and the knee).

Gentlemen of England versus the Toronto Cricket Club, c. 1870s. The rules of cricket were formalized in England in the eighteenth century, and the attempts of North Americans to change them a century later were met with criticism. As a result, ball players in the New World switched to baseball, a game whose rulebook was still in its formative stages.

Spalding's Official Rules of 1876 tackled the ambiguity of the strike zone by declaring that "every ball fairly delivered and sent into the bat over the home base and at the height called for by the batsman shall be considered a good ball." All other balls, unless swung at, were considered unfair balls and nine of these entitled the batter to first base.

In the National League, since umpires were required to warn batters on a third strike that the next one would result in a strikeout, the effective total was four. By the end of the 1870s, the warning call (and therefore the fourth strike) was eliminated. The bases-on-balls total, however, took a meandering journey from nine in 1879 to four ten years later, losing one about every second year. In 1881, the pitching distance from the mound to the home plate, which had been at forty-five feet since 1860, was pushed back a further five feet.

The current distance of sixty feet six inches was set in 1893 largely because of pitchers like Amos Rusie. The Hoosier Thunderbolt was a fearsome fastballer who threatened to turn baseball into a pitcher's game (as softball is today). Some have considered the additional six inches to have been tagged on as the result of a surveying error, but it actually resulted from the pitcher's box in 1892 being an area five and a half feet long and four feet wide, with a distance of fifty feet from the front of the box to home plate. Since the pitcher, in delivering the ball, had to keep one foot in contact with the back line of the box, the real distance at the time was fifty-five and a half feet to home plate rather than the rulebook distance of fifty feet. In 1893, the pitcher was moved back another five feet and given a pitcher's plate.

By 1884, restrictions on the pitcher's style of delivery were eliminated, in keeping with established practice. Tommy Bond's sidearm delivery had already begun to rise above the waist in the mid-1870s. The first beneficiary of the overhand delivery was Providence's Charlie Sweeney, who went from seven wins in 1883 to forty-one the next year. The last symbol of baseball's gentlemanly origins was abolished in 1887 with the removal of the batter's right to call for a high or low pitch. A formal strike zone could now be applied to all pitches.

Over the years, the strike zone has been subject to reinterpretation. Concluding that the home run was becoming all too common and thus no longer special, major-league baseball expanded the strike zone by 15 per cent in 1962 (the last significant change, in 1949, had defined the strike zone as the area between the player's knees and armpits). The effect of the expanded zone was to gradually lower pitchers' earned-run averages and to disrupt the balance between offence and defence so significantly that, in 1968, Carl Yastrzemski led the American League with a .301 average. On the field, it made a great team of the Los Angeles Dodgers with their brilliant pitching tandem of Sandy Koufax and Don Drysdale. Off the field, it bored and disillusioned fans, who deserted baseball for the spectacular offence of pro football.

By 1969, there was considerable debate as to whether baseball had a future, and in a desperate move, the strike zone was again reduced to its 1949 definition. As well, the pitcher's mound, which had been set fifteen inches higher than the level of the baselines in 1904, was lowered to ten inches. The impact was immediate—an increase of 145 home runs per inch in the 1970s—and baseball resumed its position as America's number-one sport.

In width, the present-day strike zone covers the entire area over home plate; in height, the upper level is officially supposed to be the midpoint between the top of the shoulders and pants, and the lower level, the top of the knees. According to the rules, the strike zone is to be determined from

"I can see how we won twenty-five games. What I don't understand is how he lost five"—Yogi Berra on Koufax's 1963 pitching record of 25–5.

the batter's stance when he is prepared to swing at a pitched ball. Thus, Rickey Henderson, who crouches down and uncoils as the ball is thrown, has a far more restricted strike zone than the taller Cal Ripken, who stands almost erect awaiting the pitch.

In practice, the high strike (anything above the waist) is rarely called. The reasons for this are several. Pitchers feel more secure with ground balls than with long flies and accordingly will try to keep the ball out of the batter's wheelhouse. Batters have contributed to this change by their willingness to go after lower pitches. Balls move more quickly on the artificial surfaces that were introduced in the late 1960s, encouraging contact hitters with the ability to chop the ball between the infield's defensive holes. There is also some argument that the replacement of the bulky outside protectors once worn by American League umps with the more compact inside protectors worn in the National League has, at least in the junior circuit, allowed umpires to get down lower in their crouch and thus reward pitchers for questionable deliveries at the level of the batter's knees. Frank Robinson, who in the 1960s played in both the National League with Cincinnati and the American League with Baltimore, claimed that before the discarding of the outside pad, there was a difference of two inches between the two leagues' strike zones.

With the downward drift of the American League's strike zone and the movement of players back and forth between leagues, the preponderance of opinion and spoken gossip around home plate was that the zone must be, should be, or was, falling. Umpires hearing such chatter are naturally as susceptible to suggestion as anyone else. Calls of the lower strike are not based so much on actual observation as on incremental bias. Similarly, pitchers start to throw balls lower and batters start to swing at them, laying off the high strike. Unheard from the stands is the conversation behind home plate as catcher and umpire dissect pitches. Over a period of time, all of these factors have lead to redefinition of the strike zone.

"If a catcher asks me early on if I'm planning to stay with a particular pitch," said Marty Springstead, referring to whether a low-ball strike is going to remain a strike call for the rest of the game, "I tell him, 'Well, I have so far.' Usually that's good enough for him." As early in the game as possible, the catcher takes the umpire's philosophy for that game into account. A hitter will seldom complain as long as the calls have a degree of consistency. An outside fastball is less irksome for either team if it is known early in the game whether the umpire intends to see that type of pitch as a ball or strike.

Catchers or pitchers will also bring an umpire up to date on a pitcher's changing repertoire. "There was a pitcher from Texas," Joe Sawchuk recalled, "who passed me after the first inning and said he'd just developed a new pitch. He told me to stay with it and not give up on it."

Umpires like to work with a sense of rhythm, making their calls quickly. Hesitation breeds doubt, and that can be an obstacle to good plate relations. Consequently umpires can be fooled into certain calls—for example, calling a ball when a notorious fastballer with no history of throwing the breaking ball suddenly tosses one that cuts the corner of the plate at the last moment.

The strike zone was again expanded before the 1988 season in the hope that umpires would begin calling the extinct high strike. The first casualty was the long ball. The history of baseball suggests that the impact of this change will ultimately be greater even than that of free agency.

Ironically, the umpire's judicial role has not diminished with the expansion of the rulebook. He must still interpret a pitcher's motives, deciding whether a pitch at the batter is deliberate or if it just got away from him. And the umpire must further weigh the batter's intentions if he is hit by an errant ball (under article [6.08 b], it is stipulated that if "the batter makes no attempt to avoid being touched by the ball, he is not entitled to first base but the ball is ruled dead and no runner may advance").

This is a slippery point. In 1920, Ray Chapman of the Cleveland Indians froze on a rising submarine pitch thrown by the Yankees' Carl Mays. Chapman was beaned and died later that evening, the only on-field major-league casualty in the history of the game. If one had to guess at intention, there is little doubt that Chapman would have preferred not to be hit by the ball, even though he had the opportunity to avoid it.

Sometimes the situation affects the call: in 1968 Dodger Don Drysdale not only threw more than fifty-eight consecutive scoreless innings (breaking Walter Johnson's forty-five-year record) but pitched five consecutive shutouts. Halfway through Drysdale's streak, umpire Harry Wendelstedt ruled that San Francisco's batter Dick Dietz had made no effort to get out of the way of a Drysdale throw. At the time, because the bases were loaded, the call would have ended the streak, but Dietz was given a ball and he eventually flew out.

The Wendelstedt decision suggests that obviously there are situations in which context counts, and the keen observer would argue that at least such practice is fairer than applying a long-neglected rule at a moment when it does more harm than good.

First, the case for the good. Babe Pinelli umpired in the big leagues from 1935 to 1956 and claimed not to have missed a regulation game. His last plate assignment was the fifth game of the 1956 World Series and he called

"It ain't nothin' 'til I call it"—Bill Klem, umpire, 1905–40 (second from right).

Don Larsen's ninety-seven pitches, the last being a called strike to end the only perfect game ever thrown in the Series (and the last post-season Brooklyn Dodger game in Yankee Stadium). On a one-and-two count on the last Dodger, Dale Mitchell, Larsen threw what appeared to be a high-and-outside fastball close, which Pinelli called as a strike but a rigid interpretation of the strike zone would have made a ball. Ed Runge, the ump on the right-field foul line recalled, "It took a lot of courage for him to call that last strike."

"Wasn't it a strike?" Runge was asked.

"Officially it was," he responded.

The legal definition of the strike zone provides no guidelines for situations such as the one Larsen and Pinelli faced. There is only a tacit understanding that if the ball is anywhere near the strike zone, the interpretation of the batter's stance will not only be influenced by the umpire's memory and the batter's usual pattern, but also by the pressure, passion, and history of the moment. An umpire's judgement, therefore, is based as much on his philosophy of the game as on his interpretation of the rule-book.

If a case can be made for elasticity of judgement and if we can recognize that over a period of years observed practice and ongoing discussion create subtle shifts in the interpretation of the rules, a sudden adherence to the letter of the law will seem belligerent and unfair.

Take the balk rule: runners are allowed to advance a base when "the pitcher, while touching his plate, makes any motion naturally associated with his pitch and fails to make such a delivery." The intent is to prevent the pitcher from deceiving the runner. The rule further states that "straddling the pitcher's rubber without the ball is to be interpreted as intent to deceive and ruled a balk."

In some ways, fans and players alike reacted negatively to the enforcement of the rule on balks, not because it was being unfairly applied but because the general drift of on-field action for many years had warranted a more generalized interpretation. As well, managers grumbled when umpires failed to respect context. A plodding runner on first who had never stolen a base in his career would hardly be the object of a pitcher's deception. Yet for apparently minor infractions, balks were called in 1988 in just such situations.

Nevertheless, the change was at least announced in advance and pitchers had fair warning that moves they had adopted would now be considered improper and should be modified. There is less excuse, however, for the almost draconian enforcement of the force-out rule that occurred in one of the most famous games in history.

In a late-season game in 1908, umpires Hank O'Day and Bob Emslie ruled a Giants–Cubs game no contest because the Giants' apparent winning run was nullified by Fred Merkle's failure to touch second base. It was a common occurrence for players to sprint to the locker room following a game-winning single. The alert Cubs, noticing Merkle's failure to touch second, retrieved the ball from the fans who now swarmed over the field and had the umpire apply the force-out rule long after the runner had scored and disappeared into the locker room. According to the rules, Merkle was out and the run did not count. A rematch was scheduled, which the Cubs eventually won, thus depriving the Giants of the pennant.

"I have always felt," Bill James concluded in his *Historical Baseball Abstract*, "that, if in fact it [Merkle's error in judgement] was common practice, then O'Day used very poor judgement in deciding to commence enforcement of the rule at that particular moment."

Unenforced rules, James argues, are the style of totalitarian states,

In 1956, New York Yankee pitcher Don Larsen threw the only perfect game in World Series play.

Joe Hornung of the London Tecumsehs, Canadian Champions of 1876 and 1877.

where a state official suddenly decides to toss in jail those he does not like because they have broken a law that few even remember. A statute, in short, that is not routinely enforced should not be enforceable.

That brings us to the essential issue of baseball law—that fairness must be its guiding principle. Consider that in the earliest days of the game, a fly ball was deemed caught if handled on the first bounce. This rule was aesthetically messy (why make a sincere effort at a great catch if you can draw up short and take an easy chance on the first bounce?) and restricted the runner's ability to advance, since he had to wait until he was certain that the ball had bounced at least twice. By the mid-1860s, the out on a fair bound was removed and the fly catch of fair balls adopted.

This rule worked well until the players' natural inclination to win superseded the more gentlemanly code that was in place during the 1840s. As long as comradeship and exercise were the dominant reasons for playing baseball, adherence to a code of fair play made explicit rules redundant. By the 1890s, however, ballplayers recognized that a speedy runner on first could be retired if the infielder simply allowed a relatively high pop-out to land fair. He then grabbed the ball and tossed to second for the force; the batter meanwhile would have time to reach first. In the second inning of a Chicago–Baltimore game on June 8, 1893, shortstop Bill Dahlen caught a lazy pop-fly off the bat of Joe Kelley, then dropped it and threw to second to retire the runner from first. The error was so obvious that umpire McLaughlin refused to allow the play and called the batter out even though there was nothing in the rules to prevent such misadventure. Clearly such a tactic was unfair not only because the offence was powerless to prevent it, but because, with men on first and second, such a move could easily result in a double play or, with the bases loaded, a triple play. There was some recourse for the offence. Some runners could leave base in advance in the expectation of the infielder deliberately dropping the ball while others would keep their base, but this could clearly result in a mess that no umpire wanted to handle. And so, by 1901, a new rule was in place, explicitly stating that in such cases the umpire would immediately declare an infield fly, and "that the batter would be out and runners would advance or remain at their base the same as on any fly ball."

McLaughlin's acting out of the principle of equity found codification in order that those who would not subscribe to the moral principle of fair play, as espoused by the Knickerbockers, would be required to abide by a more formal rule.

At the heart of the rulebook's interpretation is the umpire, submerged, said Furman Bisher, "in the history of baseball like idiot children in a family album".

"Umpire", a term first used in cricket, comes from the Middle English *noumper*, a third party called in to mediate in an argument between two persons. In early days, the umpire was appointed by the home team, which often led to embarrassing situations. During the Canadian championship season of 1876, a London victory over Guelph was declared no contest when it was discovered that umpire Ed Moore, a director of the Tecumsehs, had bet a box of cigars with a Montreal man that London would win. One of London's players that season, local jeweller Tom Gillean, was paid five dollars in 1879 to become one of the first independent arbiters in the National League. The umpire's lot was a lonely and uneasy one. "It is far easier," *Bryce's Canadian Base Ball Guide* for 1876 said, "to find a fitting occupant for the leading position in a first class professional nine than it is to find a suitable candidate for the onerous position of umpire." While the National League at times experimented with two umpires (the Player's League of 1890 had used two umpires, dressing them in white), they were not officially required until 1911. Before that time, runners were not reluctant to cut across the infield if the umpire wasn't looking or to grab an opponent's pants as he rounded a base. Fans naturally blamed the umpire, and assaults were not uncommon. In 1907, at Sportsman's Park, a bottle thrown by a clerk in the office of the German consul fractured the skull of umpire Billy Evans. Fans were often egged on by managers such as John McGraw, who more than once threatened to murder the game official. A third umpire was eventually added in 1933, and the fourth in 1952.

A typical game places these umpires at the centre of what is in fact a very complex and mature system of ethics. The moral philosophy of baseball holds that any deception that prevents the other side from taking appropriate action is unfair; that decisions must be lived with; that nastiness is unacceptable; that in the case of incorrect action it is the responsibility of the offended party to appeal; and that intention can be more significant than result.

A pitcher's intent in throwing at a batter informs the umpire's call, and many decisions require a similar reading. What happens, for instance, when an authorized person on the field interferes with the ball? The rule respects that person's sincere efforts to avoid the ball, but should he actually grab it, even unwillingly, the penalty is unreserved, no matter what his intentions were:

> The question of intentional or unintentional interference shall be decided on the basis of the person's actions. For example: a bat boy, ball attendant, policeman, etc., who tries to avoid being touched by the ball would be involved in unintentional interference [the ball remains alive and in play]. If, however, he kicks the ball or picks it up or pushes it, that is considered intentional interference, regardless of what his thought may have been [the ball is dead and the umpire imposes an appropriate penalty].

Consider the remarkable ways in which fairness is allied with intention. A catch is defined as the act of a fielder in getting secure possession of a ball in flight in his hand or glove and firmly holding it, providing he does not use his cap, protector, pocket, or any part of his uniform in getting possession. And then the clincher: "In establishing the validity of the catch, the fielder shall hold the ball long enough to prove he has complete control of the ball and that his release of the ball is voluntary and intentional."

Dropped fly balls are rare, but they are also open to interpretation: an unpopular decision must sometimes be made if, in the view of the umpire, the ball came loose somewhere between the time it hit the fielder's glove and was transferred to his throwing hand.

A simple rulebook would allow no room for interpretation. Regardless of situation, it would demand a specific response. In baseball, however, not everything is so clear. Spectator interference on a fly ball, for example, results in the batter's being called out and the ball declared dead. What happens, however, to a runner on third? If the fly ball is long enough, surely such a ruling would rob him of his ability to tag up and run home. The rulebook is alert to this possibility: "The umpire decides that because of the distance the ball was hit, the runner would have scored after the catch if the fielder had caught the ball which was interfered with, therefore the runner is permitted to score. This might not be the case if such fly ball was interfered with a short distance from home plate."

At times the rulebook steps beyond the purely legal to speak in the highest moral tones, a reminder of the game's gentlemanly origins. Rule

Umpire Larry Napp calls Minnie Minoso out at second as Tony Kubek applies the tag, 1960. Umpire Tim Hurst once suggested to his colleagues that they "Call 'em fast and walk away tough".

8.02(d) contains this blunt message: "To pitch at a batter's head is unsportsmanlike and highly dangerous. It should be, and is, condemned by everybody. Umpires should act without hesitation in enforcement of this rule."

Such deliberate action is treated most harshly by the rulebook. A runner, for instance, advances three bases "if a fielder deliberately touches a fair ball with his cap, mask or any part of his uniform detached from its proper place on his person." Deliberate throwing of the glove at and touching a fair ball also entitles the runner to three bases.

Baseball rules even consider the object of penalty in cases where no specific individual is identified, as in the case of an intentionally discoloured or damaged ball: "In case the umpire cannot locate the offender and if the pitcher delivers such discoloured or damaged ball to the batter, the pitcher shall be removed from the game at once and shall be suspended automatically for ten days." Stated simply, this means the player who performs the significant act is held accountable even if he has no knowledge of the transgression. It places on this athlete a burden and a responsibility that cannot be deflected by claims of ignorance.

Appeals are among baseball's unique moments. In other sports, the game official calls it as he sees it. If, for instance, a football player steps out of bounds before catching the ball, the referee does not wait for the opposition to object. He calls the play, and if he misses it, will consult with other officials. In baseball, however, a player who misses a base is not automatically called out by the umpire. Instead, he remains safe unless the opposition launches a formal appeal. To do so, the fielder in possession of the ball must touch the base with it before another pitch is made. This must be done deliberately and in consultation with the umpire. Suppose a runner missed second base on his way from first to home and that, on the same play, the hitter made it to second. Suppose further that the players on the defensive team are unaware that the runner missed second. An attempted pick-off play before the next pitch is made, in which the second baseman gets the ball while standing on second, would not constitute an appeal. The run that scored would stand, and the umpire would keep his secret to himself.

A similar situation arises when a runner tagging up on a fly ball races home before the fielder catches the ball. Again, the umpire who sees the infraction will not notify the offended team. Unless the ball is deliberately tossed to that base before the next pitch, the offence is allowed to stand and the run counts. There exists in such instances the possibility of an apparent fourth out in an inning. Consider a bases-loaded, none-out situation, where all runners leave base prior to the catch of the fly ball. The relay catches the runners from first and second before they get back to their respective bases. The third out, however, takes place after the runner from third has crossed home plate. In such a situation the run would apparently count. The obvious unfairness of a run's being credited to a team that has committed an infraction offends the very notion of fair play. And so the rules allow the team scored upon to appeal for an out on the play at third, even though three outs have already been credited.

All umpires are cautioned with the warning (one of the few printed in large letters in the rulebook), "BE IN POSITION TO SEE EVERY PLAY" and the equally important reminder, "Keep your eye everlastingly on the ball while it is in play. It is more vital to know just where a fly ball fell, or a thrown ball finished up, than whether or not a runner missed a base."

The hidden-ball trick is a delicious reminder of the complex interplay of fairness and deceit. The rules of baseball frown on wilful malfeasance. The balk rule allows runners to advance a base when the pitcher makes a pitch motion to deceive the runner. The hidden-ball trick, however, is a deception in keeping with the spirit of this rule. Not only must an umpire keep his eye on the ball but so must the runner. If the pitcher is undertaking a landscape inspection around his mound, then the runner should be leery about advancing off the base.

Hidden-ball tricks seldom work because they are so obvious. Children and major-leaguers alike will practise the faked throw to the pitcher hoping the runner jumps off the base. At the sandlot level, children will hold conferences at the mound, at which time the pitcher might slip the ball into the first baseman's glove. The ploy rarely works because its intent must be hidden from everyone but the fielder, the pitcher, and the umpire. Usually it occurs on a confusing play, perhaps one involving a run down between several bases in which a runner loses sight of the ball.

Imagine a runner rounding first on such a play, then stumbling and crawling back to first. An errant throw by the shortstop gets by the man covering first who, in this case, happens to be the pitcher. The first baseman, backing up the play, recovers the ball. In the confusion, the runner and his coach lose sight of this reversal of roles and assume that the pitcher strolling back to the mound must have the ball. No deceit has been practised and, for his part, the pitcher, if he is not straddling the rubber, is clearly not ready to make his pitch. The runner takes a step off first in preparation for a longer lead off and suddenly the first baseman slaps the glove on him, while the umpire, who has kept his eye everlastingly on the ball, signals the runner out.

Tough luck to the runner, yes; but also, within the context of the play, both fair and equitable to both sides.

Baseball tolerates the tricky or unexpected play as long as it remains

Baseball frowns on its players making a travesty of the game, but this 1883 vision of the future proved to be more fancy than fact.

within the spirit of the game. It has less respect for bad aesthetics.

A runner who, in the rulebook's words, makes "a travesty of the game" is declared out. Running the bases in reverse order for the purpose of confusing the defence is one such case. Detroit's 1907 pennant-winning year was aided by the antics of Germany Schaefer who, in a game against Cleveland, attempted to draw a throw from the catcher so that Davey Jones on third could run home. The trouble was that Schaefer was on second base, so in order to draw the throw, he raced back to first. Shortly thereafter the old "stealing first play" was banned.

Baseball guards its honour most severely, however, in its penchant for accurate statistics. A batter's average rises with a clean hit but falls if it has been aided by a fielder's error. On both plays, the batter has made first base, but the game sincerely cares about how this was done. If the batter's skill did not contribute to the result then he receives no statistical credit. In cases in which the batter walks, is hit by a pitch, or sacrifices the runner to second on a bunt, no at-bat is attributed, even though in a sacrifice bunt the batter is retired. The thinking on such plays is truly wonderful: the batter is clearly directly involved in a ball hit to, and misplayed by, a second baseman. An at-bat has occurred and an out should have taken place. That it did not in no way changes the justice of ruling statistically that the batter was out. (The new baseball statistics that record total average interestingly credit the runner with a base, assuming that some errors at least are made because a fast batter forces the defence into hurried responses.) A hit by a pitch, even though it is effectively an error on the pitcher, is clearly not a play on which the batter would have been retired. Still, there is no reason to consider it an achievement on behalf of the batter, even though some (Ron Hunt and Don Baylor, for example) have a marked ability to withstand pain by not diving away from an errant throw. The recording of no at-bat seems appropriate. A sacrifice demonstrates the morality of baseball. Such a play can hardly be credited as a hit because an out occurs. However, since the batter gives himself up to benefit the team, it would not be fair to punish him statistically.

The game's zeal for justice even overrides what many assume to be a rigid code for determining the winning pitcher. Normally, a reliever is credited with victory if he is the pitcher of record when his team assumes the lead and maintains it to the finish of the game. But there is an exception: "Do not credit a victory to a relief pitcher who is ineffective in a brief appearance, when a succeeding relief pitcher pitches effectively in helping his team maintain the lead. In such cases, credit the succeeding relief pitcher with the victory."

At its root then, this is a game that cares. Nowhere is this fact better demonstrated than in the authority vested in the umpire and official scorer to render what is appropriate in the situation, using the rulebook only as a guide.

Take a case in which a fielder interferes with the runner in the fielding of a ball. "It is entirely up to the judgement of the umpire as to whether a fielder is in the act of fielding a ball." The example that the rulebook provides is guarded in its claim to certainty: if an infielder dives at a ground ball that passes him and continues to lie on the ground, delaying the runner's progress, "he very likely has obstructed the runner."

"Very likely" as a guiding principle tosses the umpire back into the clutches of Rule 9.01(c): "Each umpire has authority to rule on any point not specifically covered in these rules." Common sense as an ultimate arbiter may be deeply troubling for those looking for rulebook chapter and verse, but the humbling responsibility implied may be the one real reason that baseball has flourished in very different times and places.

INNING 4

GREATEST HITS

Bill Veeck, major-league team owner between the 1940s and 1970s, fondly recalled that his childhood idols, the National League Cubs, "were mostly drunks off the field and craftsmen on it."

Skill sets the professional ballplayer apart from the crowd, not the cut of his uniform, not the size of his contract, not even his willingness to model underwear. Such skill is proven in the ability to get around on a terrifying 95-mile-per-hour fastball, to take a deceptive breaking ball that falls out of the strike zone, to make the perfect throw to first base from deep in the hole at shortstop. There is, of course, the element of having the right genes. Lads like Mike Epstein who grow up to be 6' 3 1/2" tall and weigh 230 pounds have obvious advantages over those like Albie Pearson who weigh in at 140 pounds. In Brendan Boyd and Fred Harris's tongue-in-cheek book on baseball cards (*The Great American Baseball Card Flipping, Trading and Bubble Gum Book*), they note that had Pearson been six inches taller, he would have reached almost 5' 11".

Big-league scouts will acknowledge that they look for size, strength, and athletic ability in a player. All the desire and effort in the world cannot substitute for those assets.

Nevertheless, Albie Pearson still pieced together nine years in the majors, from 1958 to 1966, with stops in Washington and Baltimore, before finding steady employment with the expansion Los Angeles Angels. In that time, he compiled a respectable .270 average, though one might have expected an outfielder to contribute more than his twenty-eight career roundtrippers. Mike Epstein, for all his advantages in size, actually played in eighty-one fewer regular-season games in his nine major-league seasons between 1966 and 1974 than did Pearson. Though Epstein hit only .244, his streaks were plentiful enough to count for 130 home runs in Baltimore, Washington, Oakland, Texas, and California. He is remembered, however, for one World Series appearance for Oakland in 1972 when he managed no hits in sixteen official at-bats. That record was redeemed only slightly by five bases on balls. He could look back at least with some comfort to others' comparable streaks, such as those of Chicago Cubs' Jimmy Sheckard, who amassed a zero-for-twenty-one record in the 1906 World Series, matched by similarly frustrated rival Billy Sullivan of the crosstown White Sox in the same series.

The baseball pantheon houses four types of gods—the great star, the everyday player, the man off the street, and the team player given heroic stature by one magnificent achievement.

Opposite: During ceremonies marking the twenty-fifth anniversary of Yankee Stadium, June 13, 1948, Babe Ruth's No. 3 was permanently retired.

Great stars are generally remembered long after their day has passed. When Willie Stargell entered baseball's Hall of Fame in Cooperstown, New York, in 1988, he was the 200th individual chosen for admittance.

In lionizing the great star, it is easy to forget the human dimensions of the game: even in Ted Williams's exhilarating 1941 season when he batted .406 (the last major leaguer to bat over .400) and had an on-base average of over .500, he still popped up, flew out, bounced out, and struck out twenty-seven times for a failure rate of six out of ten official at-bats. In his only World Series appearance for the Red Sox in 1946, his batting average of .200 included no extra base hits. As a manager with Washington and then the transplanted Texas Rangers, he produced a team record that descended annually—from a high of eighty-six wins in 1969 to a sorrowful fifty-four in 1972.

The drama of Ted Williams's career is aptly summed up in his last at-bat. The "Splendid Splinter" homered and, with head bowed, made his circuit of the bases. He would not acknowledge the cries for a curtain call that echoed through Fenway Park, a plaintive request that John Updike captured in a story about this game, "Hub Fans Bid Kid Adieu". Williams was a complex personality who had disdain for a defensive, hit-to-all-fields batting style and preferred to concentrate on driving the ball to right field. His crusade for the dramatic hitting style was a measure of his star status: he had a philosophy of the game and espoused it through achievement.

The fascination with the great star is not a new phenomenon. Babe Ruth was a national hero in America between the wars. More sainted than saintly, Ruth live a scandal-sheet life that perhaps should have deprived him of mainstream allure. Such has been the fascination of baseball that players' public peccadilloes are gently washed away as honest mistakes. Ruth's appetite for what the papers called "the fancy lady" was legendary, though reporters generally ignored his wandering ways. In an exhibition tour with Ruth in 1920, Ping Bodie is reported to have said, "I don't room with him. I room with his suitcase."

John Drebinger of *The New York Times* called Ruth "the most uninhibited human being I have ever known". Yet Jimmy Breslin called him the only sports legend "who completely lived up to advance billing". While Ruth could play the celebrity role, and did so on occasions when he took to the stage, he was simply too much in love with baseball to place himself above its more humbling experiences. In 1938, when he no doubt could have been happily retired in comfort as the game's grand old man, he was coaching for the Brooklyn Dodgers. Torontonian Goody Rosen, just starting with the Dodgers in 1938, tells the story of how he and Ruth trapped a player who was stealing the great one's cigars: "The Babe accused me," Rosen recalled, "but I said I wouldn't have any use for his stogies, so we got some firecrackers and put one in the end of each of the Babe's cigars. We wrapped them and put them on his shelf. On the train to Boston that night I spotted our catcher Babe Phelps with a bunch of cigars in his front pocket. He was about to light up and I gave Ruth the sign. He ran in just in time for the damnedest explosion you ever heard. Ruth wanted to be mad at him but couldn't stop laughing."

A truly great star is one who never, even at the peak of his popularity, discounts or dismisses his fans. He is, in short, not famous for being famous, but for excelling in a game most fans have played at some time in their lives and demonstrating superior team skills as well as personal ones.

Joe DiMaggio has remained for more than thirty-five years since his

"In 1955 there was 77,263,127 male American human beings. And every one of them...would have given two arms, a leg and his collection of Davy Crockett iron-ons to be Teddy Ballgame"—Boyd and Harris (1973) on Ted Williams.

Bobby Thomson's "shot heard 'round the world" won the 1951 pennant for the New York Giants.

retirement the game's great romantic figure. Popular songs by, among others, Simon and Garfunkel, have expanded his myth, and his post-career marriage to Marilyn Monroe further enhanced his public image. He will be remembered longest, however, for his fifty-six-consecutive-game hitting streak in 1941. Harvard professor and author Stephen Jay Gould refers to this baseball accomplishment as "so many standard deviations above the expected distribution that it should not have happened at all....Joe DiMaggio accomplished what no other ballplayer had done. He beat the hardest taskmaster of all, a woman who makes Nolan Ryan's fastball look like a cantaloupe in slow motion—lady luck." But to an entire generation of fans, that 1941 streak is immortal because it formed part of America's public dialogue as the country prepared for war. Thus, what is on one level a relatively meaningless statistic became on another a kind of benchmark to remind people where they were and what they were doing during that period.

So mythic has this accomplishment become that, in researching his book *Streak,* author Michael Seidel discovered numerous instances where players recalled events that never occurred—almost as if they felt the need to match the feat's heroism. One that Seidel missed was Phil Marchildon's account of game forty-six. Marchildon remembered that DiMaggio was fed a diet of unhittable curve balls all afternoon, but finally, in his last at-bat, he hit a home run on a supposedly wasted high fastball, with two strikes against him. It's a lovely story except that Joe actually connected in the first inning.

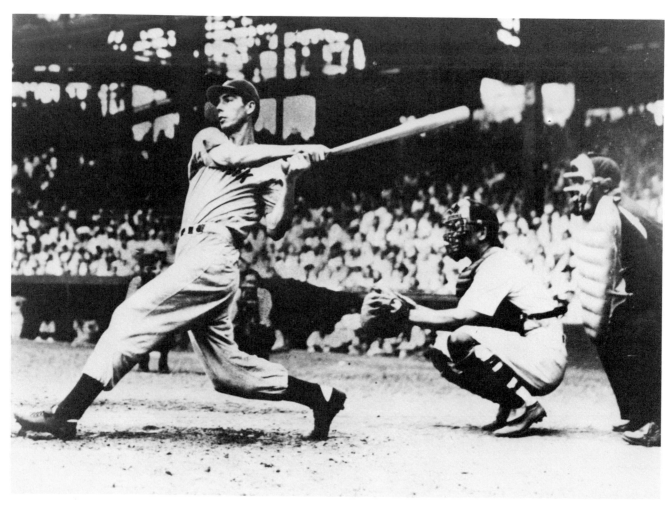

"Joe DiMaggio batting sometimes gave the impression—the sugges-tion—that the old rules and dimensions of baseball no longer applied to him, and that the game had at last grown unfairly easy"— Roger Angell (1972).

Lou Gehrig's fame, in contrast, rests on a double curse. Despite his batting statistics (a .340 career average and 493 home runs) and a longevity record of 2,130 consecutive games, which would have made him a great star in any other baseball era, he was overshadowed by Babe Ruth and did not gain supremacy, even on his own team, until late in his career. Fate cruelly dogged Gehrig: his greatest day, June 3, 1932, on which he hit four home runs in a game, was stolen by the news of John McGraw's resigna-tion as manager of the Giants. In Gehrig's retirement speech at Yankee Stadium in 1939, he noted: "Today I consider myself the luckiest man on the face of the earth. I might have been given a bad break but I've got an awful lot to live for." His premature death at the age of thirty-seven from an incurable muscular disorder, amyotrophic lateral sclerosis, so affected the public that Gehrig, like DiMaggio, entered the public consciousness, but in a tragic way: ALS is now known simply as Lou Gehrig's Disease.

Some stars, though their public profile has diminished over time, remain, within the game's heritage, the stuff of legend. Bill James, popular analyst of baseball strategy, rates Walter Johnson as the greatest right-hander in terms not only of his peak value but also of his career. Known for his decency, charm, and style, Johnson lived in fear that one of his fastballs would one day kill a man; but, said Ty Cobb, "You never had to worry about a curve in those days from Walter, or a change of pace. Just speed, raw speed, blinding speed, too much speed." In Johnson's greatest season, 1913, he won 36 games, had an earned-run average of 1.09, and struck out 243 while walking only 38. And his career record of 416–279, which included 3,508 strikeouts and 110 shutouts, leaves one wondering what he might have achieved with a better team than the Washington Senators.

Then there are the great stars who leave no awesome record or stunning individual achievement but are ideal team players. For much of the 1950s, and all of the 1960s and early 1970s, Al Kaline was synonymous with the Detroit franchise. A ten-time recipient of the Gold Glove and a five-time *Sporting News* American League all-star, he was a patient slugger credited with 399 home runs and 1,277 walks. Bill James rated Kaline sixth among all-time right fielders, a list that includes Ruth and Hank Aaron in the number-one and number-two positions. Of Kaline, baseball historian

"He was the guy who hit all those home runs the year Ruth broke the record"—Franklin P. Adams, columnist, 1948, on Lou Gehrig, pictured below (left) with Babe Ruth (right).

Douglas Wallop said: "He has left the mark of neither a Cobb nor a DiMaggio. Few players have. Instead, he has been merely excellent." Though a thirty-three-year-old veteran in his only World Series in 1968, Kaline led Detroit to victory with eleven hits, of which two were home runs. His game-winning, bases-loaded single in the seventh inning of game five prevented Detroit's elimination and set the stage for their dramatic comeback in St. Louis.

Finally, there are the stars with the touch of wonder. Of Willie Mays, Leo Durocher said, "He could do the five things you have to do to be a superstar: hit, hit with power, run, throw, and field. And he had a magic ingredient that turns a superstar into a super superstar—he lit up the room when he came in." A one-time member of the Birmingham Black Barons, Mays was the toast of New York, particularly after his sensational catch in the 1954 World Series. His basket-type catches earned him eleven Gold Gloves as a leading fielder and, besides Hank Aaron, he is the only player to have hit five hundred or more home runs and collected three thousand or more hits. A perennial all-star team member (twenty-four times), he was the first player to hit a home run and steal a base in the same all-star game.

Free agency and the spectacle of salary negotiations have, of course, tarnished the image of the great star and have made virtually every player a celebrity. Players and, perhaps ironically, owners have benefited from the shift in the motivation to play from magic to money as the game now attracts spectators in record numbers. However, money has also changed stars in less obvious ways. In Brooklyn in the 1950s, players such as Duke Snider or Pee Wee Reese lived in the neighbourhood and walked to the park, sharing small talk with the locals. A 1979 *Sports Illustrated* story described a writer/fan attempting to find the home of Don Sutton and succeeding only in becoming lost in the blind alleys and dead-end streets that ply the hills around Los Angeles. Where at one time, when the season was over, players as hugely successful as Ruth would hit the barnstorming trail, travelling by train to greet the public in out-of-the-way places, they now fly first class and have little contact with the public. Yesterday's stars were no less taken with their own status; they were just somehow more available.

If the great star as celebrity threatens to confound our view of baseball, so does the equally vapid trend of obsession with the trivial. At this level, fandom does not discriminate, and extends to the least-stellar members of the profession. It is fun, of course, to ask who was the third baseman of the famous Tinker-to-Evers-to-Chance infield for the National League Chicago Cubs. The answer: Harry Steinfeldt, a fourteen-year National League veteran with Cincinnati, Chicago, and Boston from 1898 to 1911, forgotten largely because of popular lyricist Franklin Adams's doggerel about the saddest of all possible words being Tinker to Evers to Chance.

The modern mania for baseball trivia serves as a reminder, perhaps, that it *is* just a game. The seventh edition of the *Baseball Encyclopedia*, a 2,875-page record of the game's statistics, is the ultimate tribute, either to the game's fundamental meaninglessness or to the worth of every action that ever took place on any field. Any man who plays one inning in the majors has a tiny portion of his life immortalized as a flicker in the on-going coverage of the game. So poignant are some of these tiny moments that occasionally one is elevated from fact to be honoured in fiction. Such is the case in W.P. Kinsella's treatment of Moonlight Graham in his novel *Shoeless Joe*. Born Archibald Wright Graham in Fayetteville, North Carolina, Moonlight died on August 25, 1965, in Chisholm, Minnesota. He

"There's only one way to time [Walter] Johnson's fastball; when you see the arm start forward—swing"—Birdie McCree, New York Highlanders' executive, 1908.

Willie Mays, greeted at home plate by Don Mueller (22) and Monte Irvin (20).

batted left, threw right, stood 5′ 10 1/2″, weighed 170 pounds, played one game for the New York Giants in 1905, and was credited with no official at-bat. Yet, there he is, alive within the unfolding picture of the game.

Earl Cook, from Lemonville, Ontario, for most of his life a hardworking farmer on the outskirts of Toronto, took time to play baseball during his rural career: from Toronto to Beckley to Syracuse to Buffalo to Knoxville, Beaumont, and Portland, from 1932 to 1944—all minor-league play, except for two innings in a 1941 game with Detroit when he struck out one man and allowed four hits. Cook remembered the long train trips out of Toronto on Saturday night to play Baltimore on Sunday because the Canadian city forbade commercial play on the sabbath, and he remembered ballplayers cooling their feet in a tub of icewater between innings of a Texas League game. Over those years, he won 101 and lost 124, a record omitted from his entry in the *Baseball Encyclopedia*.

Many of the brief portraits contained there are oddly incomplete. John Moore Baxter—date of birth in Spokane, Washington, unknown; resting place, likewise—played six inconsequential games at first base for the Cardinals in 1907, batting a sad .190. Five years later, according to his encyclopedia entry, he was deported from Canada for bootlegging; there, his baseball trail runs dry. The end of the trail for Dodger Len Koenecke is, on the other hand, duly documented. In mid-September 1935, the temperamental three-year veteran chartered a plane from Detroit to Buffalo and, near Toronto, had drunk himself into an ugly dispute with the co-pilot. Koenecke was cooled out with a fire extinguisher, and by the time the plane landed in Long Branch, on the outskirts of Toronto, his career average of .297 was confirmed for all time.

The everyday ballplayer, such as those noted above, was guaranteed a good income while it lasted; however, the cost was a nomadic lifestyle and a desperate urgency born of an uncertain future. Few players had fallback positions as handsome as those of two nineteenth-century players, John Montgomery Ward of the New York Giants with his brilliant legal career, and Billy Sunday of the Chicago National League team, who earned even greater fame as a charismatic evangelist. More representative of the nomadic, financially insecure ballplayer of the period was Scott Hastings, whose accredited major-league career ran from 1871 to 1877, with stops in Rockford, Cleveland, Baltimore, Hartford, Chicago, Louisville, and Cincinnati. His letters in the late winter of 1877 to Guelph Maple Leaf owner George Sleeman reveal the coldly realistic attitude that many players may have found it necessary to adopt: "I can not bring my wife along with me as she will not be able to get out of the room by the 1st, let alone travelling which would be dangerous at this time of year. And especially so in going still further north. She would be almost sure to have a relapse, so I will let her stay until the latter part of May at home with her mother. I would prefer to board at a private house but I will have plenty of time to make all arrangements before she comes. Now Mr. Sleeman, for the, 'to me', disagreeable part of this letter. When you send me my money, start it about next Saturday or Monday the 26th at the farthest as I wish to make a few arrangements before I leave. And I wish you could make it a little more than it was last time if you would be so kind—I will have to leave some of it with my wife, of course, and after I have paid my fare and other travelling expenses, I don't think I will have quite enough to buy and stock a farm."

Hastings was to live thirty more years, settling eventually in Sawtelle, California, but beyond that, the encyclopedia is silent.

Although Wyman Andrus from Orono, Ontario, does not as yet have an entry in the encyclopedia, there is some evidence that he left his Hamilton team in late summer of 1885 to find employment in the United States and was conscripted for Providence's National League lineup on September 15. (*The Sporting Life*'s boxscore says that Wally Andrews played that game but newspaper accounts, then as now, often seem to sacrifice accuracy to meet deadlines.) Andrus was a schoolteacher in the off season, in such places as Newtonville, Ontario, but each summer through the 1880s he ventured to such places as Portland (Maine), Buffalo, St. Louis, Indianapolis, and Hamilton to play pro ball. A speedy third baseman who often batted in the leadoff spot and generally had impressive statistics, Andrus has no file card in the minor-league list maintained in the Baseball Hall of Fame. He eventually graduated from medical school at the University of Toronto and practised in Miles City, Montana, where he was mayor for twelve years; when he died in 1935, he left no mention of his major-league career. Perhaps the eighth edition of baseball's Domesday Book will do so.

In setting out to quantify with statistical precision that which can never be adequately recorded other than in its daily re-creation on a ball field, the encyclopedia offers a record of achievement dating back to 1871 in a measurable form unique to the game.

The alphabetic record for 1876 to the present (1871 to 1875 belongs to

When Ralph Houk made Al Kaline a designated hitter in 1974, a local critic wrote: "He is taking from me— all of us in Detroit—one of the great joys of our life...we don't have too much in Detroit—one good theater, one London Chop House, one Windsor Tunnel and one right fielder. He is taking our right fielder away from us and summer in the city may never be the same again."

"Sportsmanship and easy going methods are all right, but it is the prospect of a hot fight that brings out the crowds"—John McGraw, New York Giants' manager, 1902–32.

the National Association) begins with the great star, Hank Aaron, originally scouted in Buffalo by Dewey Griggs of the Boston Braves on the recommendation of Jimmy Wilkes of the barnstorming Indianapolis Clowns. Eventually Aaron was brought up to the big leagues in 1954, one year after the team became the Milwaukee Braves, and he followed the Braves to Atlanta, where they moved in 1966. Aaron finally settled in 1975 for two seasons with the Milwaukee Brewers (a transfer team from Seattle). His home run total of 755 is untouched in North America, though several years ago it was surpassed in the Japan League by Sadaharu Oh. Aaron stands third in games played, second in at-bats, third in hits, eighth in doubles, second in runs scored, and first in RBI on the all-time lists.

The last name in the encyclopedia's pitcher register is George Zuverink, an everyday player who reached the bigs in the 1950s and whose totals (including thirty-two wins and thirty-six losses) don't win him a place on any all-time list, even though, in 1956, he led the American League in games saved, a statistical category that had not yet been acknowledged. This reliever retired to the insurance business, while Hank Aaron found a place in the Atlanta Braves' organization.

Occasionally the door opens to let in an anomaly—the man off the street, who by some fluke or strange event crosses the line between

everyday life and the mythological proportions of a place in the official
baseball story. Such an opportunity was provided by the game's greatest
hitter, Ty Cobb, whose career total of 4,191 hits (subject, as always, to
revision when new research reveals Cobb hits erroneously credited
elsewhere) was finally surpassed by Pete Rose in 1985.

(Cobb may also have been the game's meanest man; his ugly tempera-
ment disgusted even his own teammates. Such was his status, however,
that even though damaging information in the 1920s revealed that he had
been involved in fixing games, Cobb was exonerated by Commissioner
Landis—the man who, a few years earlier, barred Buck Weaver from the
game simply for having known of, even though he refused to take part in,
Chicago's throwing of the 1919 World Series.)

In a 1912 game, Cobb jumped over the rail of the wooden stands at
New York's Highlander Park and took several punches at an abusive fan
who, as it happened, was a minor local politician. League president Ban
Johnson, who had founded the American League from an assemblage of
teams originally based in the midwest in the 1890s, suspended the superstar. Fellow players took Cobb's side, sympathizing perhaps with his
response to such provocation, and refused to play a Saturday, May 17,
game in Philadelphia. The desperate Tiger management hastily recruited a

At the end of Hank Aaron's twenty-three-year major-league career, he had accumulated 3,771 hits, and 755 home runs, scored 2,174 runs, and driven in 2,297 runs.

Pete Rose slides into third base, 1972. Between 1963 and 1986, Charlie Hustle played in more major-league games (3,562), had more at-bats (14,053), and got more hits (4,256) than anyone else in baseball history.

team of Philadelphia semi-pros and members of the St. Joseph's College team. One of the players was a future priest, Aloysius Joseph Travers, whose career total would consist of this one game in which he allowed 26 hits and 7 bases on balls and departed with a 15.75 earned-run average. Errors and Philadelphia's need to bat in only eight innings helped keep down Travers's totals.

One year earlier, an even more outrageous invasion of the diamond occurred, of somewhat less benefit to the recruit. New York Giants' manager John McGraw, who appears perennially unhappy in every photo taken of him, allowed the team's mascot, Charles Victory Faust, to pitch in several innings in the 1911 season. McGraw was one of the game's great managers. In his thirty-three-year career, he led the Giants to nine World Series appearances; losing six of them may have contributed to his sour disposition. When Faust, a man of limited intelligence who had tried to convince McGraw that his play would lead the Giants to victory, failed his tryout, McGraw allowed him to stay around as a good-luck charm. This period was one of baseball's least enlightened ones. Willing blacks were conscripted as mascots, dressed in gaudy outfits by major-league squads who would rub their hair for good luck. Hunchbacks, such as Louis Van Zeldt with the Philadelphia Athletics, and the mentally handicapped were trained for similar purposes.

Late in the 1911 season, Faust had a turn at pitching, and the Boston Braves shared in the absurdity of the situation by intentionally making three outs.

Unusual recruitment policies extended beyond mascots. In 1945, as the quality of wartime ball reached new depths, the St. Louis Browns passed on picking up any of the available gifted black players, banned by baseball's unwritten segregation code, and opted for one-armed outfielder

Pete Gray. Pitcher Oscar Judd of the Philadelphia National League team (known that season as the Blue Jays) called Gray a joke, "a man who couldn't get around on my fast ball. I felt bad pitching to him." In fairness to Gray, however, he was far from a joke. He had had an uneven minor-league career in organized baseball and was a legitimate talent, although it is unlikely that he would have made the majors in anything other than wartime. In 77 games, he tallied 51 hits, for a .218 average. (Interestingly, the 1988 United States Olympic baseball team's lineup included a one-armed pitcher, Jim Abbott, considered by many to be one of the best prospects in all of baseball.)

Some player choices were simply outrageous. Eddie Gaedel's one-line entry in the encyclopedia, which describes him as 3' 7", 65 pounds, seems to be a typesetter's hijinks. Did the Browns sink so low as to allow a child to play for them? In fact, Eddie was a midget signed by Bill Veeck as a rather cheap publicity stunt. Wearing number 1/8, Gaedel made his one pinch-hitting appearance in the second game of the August 19, 1951, doubleheader against the Detroit Tigers and walked on four straight balls. Veeck had warned Gaedel that if he dared swing at a pitch a gunman on the roof would shoot him. The idea of bringing a midget to bat was probably inspired by James Thurber's story "You Could Look It Up"; the idea of a sniper to keep him in line might have come to him from the story of Lou McLane, a hunchback hired by Connie Mack's As, who fell in with bootleggers and was gunned down in a gangland war.

There was some controversy following Gaedel's appearance over the inclusion of such an obviously bizarre incident in the official baseball record, but a love of the incongruous prevailed and provided fans for all time with yet another perspective on the game's rich history.

St. Louis baseball writer Bob Broeg remembered his interview with Gaedel: "I said to him that he's what I wanted always to be, an ex–big leaguer. He suddenly jumped down, thrust out his chest and seemed very proud of himself. Then he shook hands and was gone. I never saw him again."

Gaedel died from shock after being mugged in Chicago ten years later, and his mother was later swindled out of his uniform by a man posing as a representative from the Hall of Fame. Gaedel's moment of glory survives in a photograph and a stat.

Historian John Holway notes that the Fausts and the Van Zeldts (and perhaps, by extension, Eddie Gaedel) were products of an age in baseball when superstition was as important as talent in the formula for pennant success. It was a time, too, when literature and myth were the bottom line. When the Braves conspired with the Giants in the Faust affair, they brought theatre to the game, suggesting that somewhere in the seriousness of play there was a place for the absurd and humorous. That special place seems to get smaller each year.

In modern times, when every player is a star, it is sometimes forgotten that ballplayers are fundamentally human and that it is the game and its record keeping that elevates them to the mythical. Bobby Thomson of the New York Giants was a dependable though by no means spectacular fifteen-year, major-league veteran, with a career batting average of .270 with 264 home runs. He would be memorable for the sturdiness and honesty of his play alone, were it not for one incredible moment on October 3, 1951, in the final playoff game between the Giants and the Brooklyn Dodgers.

The Thomson saga is proof that the elements of storytelling play as significant a role as analytical record keeping in the history of the game. The score of the game stands at 5–4 for the Giants, with Thomson provid-

Rocky Nelson may have been a major-league journeyman, but in the minor leagues he was a star, first in Montreal and then in Toronto, in the 1950s.

Jackie Robinson's stolen-base total never surpassed 40 in the regular season but just the threat of his speed alarmed enemy pitchers.

ing the game-winning home run with two men on base in the bottom of the ninth inning. A whole season preceded the game and the World Series between the Giants and the New York Yankees followed it, but hardly anyone except a Yankee fan recalls the series. It is the season that led up to October 3, 1951, that lives on in legend, a fitting prologue to an epic tale that popular mythologizers have called the "Miracle of Coogan's Bluff". Bobby Thomson's game-winning drive was impressive but not impossible. He had, in fact, been rather successful against Dodger pitcher Ralph Branca. And while the Dodgers had squandered a 13 1/2-game lead with only 44 games remaining, Jackie Robinson had saved the season for Brooklyn with a great catch and a home run on the last day of regular play. (Such fat-from-the-fire occurrences are not isolated in the game's history: in the 1978 season, the Yankees came from fourteen games out to catch Boston, only to see the Red Sox fight back from three games out to tie for first on the last day of play.)

What made a myth of 1951 was the advent of television during the Dodgers–Giants rivalry, one of the greatest in baseball. The confluence of these factors has created a special moment in baseball memory that has become a kind of statement about the mystical relationship of the game and its fans. In short, 1951 was a magic season because the public agreed to think and talk about it that way—and continues to do so.

In a 1980 "M*A*S*H" episode, Winchester bankrolls Klinger's prediction that the 1951 Dodgers will defeat the Giants, and as the season unfolds, the audience watches with delighted anticipation the undoing of the self-assured doctor. In the stageplay *Same Time Next Year*, radio announcer Russ Hodges's recorded banshee shriek "The Giants win the pennant! The Giants win the pennant! The Giants win the pennant!", which filled the air long after the winning blow was struck, is all that is needed to tell the audience what year it is.

Strictly speaking, it is probably inappropriate to refer to the Thomson home run as myth, magic, or miracle. However, as a way to describe the meaning of the 1951 season and the status it has been given among sporting events of this century, those words seem oddly appropriate.

Such language pervades any discussion of the great and not-so-great moments and players in baseball. It could hardly be otherwise, given the game's stature in North American popular culture. Since its modernization in New York City in the 1840s, the game has had enormous significance for successive generations, and the cumulative burden of responsibility to the fans is sometimes difficult to bear for the players.

Miller Huggins, whose batting average had been in decline for the past four seasons, surrendered his second-base post in 1916 with these words: "You asked me some time ago when I would call it a career as a player; well, my public gave you the answer this afternoon. You've seen the last of Miller Huggins as this club's second baseman."

It was astute of Huggins to call the hometown fans "my public"; the term has connotations of civility, judgement, and community that are lacking in the one-dimensional "fans" or the even lonelier "crowd". Perhaps recognizing this, Larry Bowa, a Philadelphia Phillie throughout

Hall of Famer Pee Wee Reese was team leader and shortstop of the great Brooklyn Dodgers in the 1940s and 1950s. Roger Kahn dubbed those teams "the Boys of Summer".

"There isn't enough mustard in the whole world to cover that hot dog"—Darold Knowles, Oakland pitcher, on Reggie Jackson, 1974.

the 1970s, told his reticent teammate, pitcher Steve Carlton, that he had an obligation to talk to the media and, through them, to the larger audience: "Baseball is a public game," he said. "We owe them something."

"It's our game," answered Carlton. "We only owe them our performance." For Carlton, Thomas Boswell noted, baseball had become "a private game of catch."

The Babe, as any fan knows, would have given a different response. The man whom sportswriter Jimmy Cannon called "a parade all by himself" and of whom writer Roger Kahn said, "As he moved, center stage moved with him," might have been, under the weight of media attention, as surly, uncooperative, and resentful of the public as are some celebrities today. However, it is more likely that Ruth, like Toronto's Jesse Barfield or Pittsburgh's Jim Gott, would have retained his warm and good-humoured connection to the "common man". It was that mantle that he brought to the game.

THE SCIENTIFIC METHOD

In analysing the reasons for the dearth of .400 hitters from major-league lineups since Ted Williams last achieved the feat in 1941, Harvard professor Stephen Jay Gould argued convincingly that the most significant cause appeared to be a withering of the more extreme variations in batting averages. All creatures, including ballplayers, adapt to the challenges of their environments and successful coping mechanisms, once remarkable, are eventually adopted by all and become the norm.

League averages from 1961 to 1980 were virtually the same as for the period 1901 to 1920, during which the .400 hitter and his near cousin, the plus .380 hitter, were relatively common. In 1911, Ty Cobb and Joe Jackson batted .420 and .408, respectively. The relative extinction of the gifted .400 performer is not a sign that ability has declined or that the more talented have opted for careers in banking or pro football; rather, it marks the evolution of a breed of skilled pitchers and fielders. And while the average level of batting performance has remained relatively constant, the edges that the truly superior star could exploit (remember Wee Willie Keeler's axiom that he could hit them where they ain't) have diminished, eliminating extremes of achievement. Baseball, Gould concluded, has become a science in its ability to repeat and duplicate precision in its execution.

There is something salutary about evidence that baseball's long march forward has taken it beyond the realm of magic and into the apparently more rational one of science. It is equally satisfying, however, to observe in baseball an attempt to turn science back into a form of magic.

Scientific issues have been part of the learned study of sport since we first started taking games seriously as something other than childhood revels or sacred ritual. Such study has in fact often retarded the progress of sport. Expert opinion considered it physically impossible to ride a two-wheeled bicycle until well into the 1860s. In horse racing, there was lengthy debate on the question of whether all four feet of a galloping horse were off the ground at the same time. By proving that they were, California's Governor Stanford collected on a $50,000 bet in 1878. Even more acrimonious discussion centred on whether a curve ball actually curved. The curve, the most devilish of pitching deliveries in baseball, causes even the most confident power hitter to wither and write home, "Dear Mom. They started throwing curves. Will be home Friday."

The pitch was supposedly invented in 1863 by a fourteen-year-old Brooklyn youngster, Bill Cummings. He practised throwing clamshells in his backyard and found that by gripping first the clam and later a ball

Opposite: In 1988, combining speed with power, Jose Canseco of Oakland became the first major-leaguer to hit over 40 home runs (42) and steal 40 bases in a season. He was a long way, however, from the record set by Len Tucker in the 1956 season of the Class-B Southwestern League during which Tucker hit 51 homers and stole 47 bases.

firmly with the middle finger and snapping the wrist to make it break down and away from the direction it was thrown, a curving action occurred.

Many disputed the possibility of the curving action and so, in 1870, Henry Chadwick set up a rather unusual laboratory. Two poles were placed forty-five feet apart, with a third pole halfway between them, all in a direct line. The experiment called for pitcher Fred Goldsmith, standing on the left side of the chalkline, to throw the ball so that it crossed the line, rounded the centre pole, and returned to the left side from which it was thrown before reaching the last pole. Goldsmith performed the feat half a dozen times and "proved to countless spectators," Chadwick wrote, "that a sphere could cheat natural laws.... What had been an optical illusion now is an established fact."

The pitch was still technically forbidden in match play but the repeal in 1872 of an old rule prohibiting pitchers from snapping their wrists allowed for its legal use.

The curve ball was a sensation, and by the end of 1877, *The New York Clipper* noted, "Club managers the past season got into quite a furor about engaging curve pitchers especially those of the class whose forte was great speed as well as the curve. They seemed to turn up their noses at any man who 'hadn't got the curve' as well as the nerve. Moreover this class of managers went in for a curve pitcher without any regard to the necessity of having also a splendid catcher to back him up."

The curve ball proved to be the undoing of at least one franchise. In 1878, the London Tecumsehs went to Fred Goldsmith on practically every occasion and, when his arm and side tightened up in mid-season, the perplexed London management accused him and his teammates of deliberately losing games. Instead of respecting the demands this new pitch was placing on their pitcher in the way of increased outings, the Tecumsehs simply fired all of their American professionals, suddenly tumbled in the International Association standings, and at season's end quietly withdrew from the league.

What Goldsmith and Chadwick had apparently proved in 1870 and what countless batters confessed to be real was temporarily challenged in 1941. A curve ball in flight was photographed with the use of high-speed strobes by *Life* magazine. "This standby of baseball [may be], after all, only an optical illusion," they concluded. Twelve years later, claiming improved photographic techniques, the magazine reversed its verdict. Today, it is acknowledged that a good and deliberate curve can deviate by more than a foot from a straight line.

A baseball curves naturally because it spins and has a raised surface of stitching. Air cannot go through the ball so it goes above or below. Greater pressure exists on one side of the ball, causing it to veer in the opposite direction where the pressure is less. By spinning the ball clockwise, a southpaw's pitch curves away from a left-handed batter. A counterclockwise spin creates a screwball, which curves towards the same batter. This principle was understood in the 1870s and instructions were printed on how to bring the pitch either onto the batter's fists or out of his reach. Christy Mathewson threw a successful screwball dubbed the "fadeaway" because it appeared to dive inside the batter rather than across the plate. Giants pitcher Carl Hubbell made the screwball his bread-and-butter pitch in the 1930s.

Almost from the first, baseball was much taken with the application of scientific and industrial models. When *The New York Clipper* first remarked on the game's growth on November 22, 1856, it said baseball "bids fair to become a formidable rival to the more scientific game of cricket". While

Game in London, Ontario, 1876, between the local Tecumsehs and the Chicago Mutuals.

His base-path and fielding speed earned Joe DiMaggio the moniker "The Yankee Clipper", after the speedy Boston–to–New York train. Yankee teammates called him simply "Cruiser".

there is little evidence to suggest that employers saw the game as a device to control workers (in fact, unions of shoemakers were among the first to adopt it as a way of providing fraternal comfort to their members), the game was ideally suited to the emerging industrial ideology of the nineteenth century. As a moral force, baseball, according to Ralph Waldo Emerson, taught "honesty, pragmatism and appreciation of earned merit". The game helped train players in attitudes useful for work. It encouraged specialization and division of labour and showed how applied science could lead to practical and quantifiable results.

Frederick Winslow Taylor, the father of scientific management in the industrial setting, was convinced that time-and-motion studies of workers would reveal the best way to perform all tasks. His theories bolstered the introduction of assembly-line production. (Ironically, Taylor was credited with introducing overhand pitching while he was a student at Tufts University in the 1870s and declared it to be a scientific improvement to his performance.) Industrial strategists noted that baseball accommodated itself to the tyranny of time and actually allowed men to operate within its constraints.Thus, it was more to be favoured than cricket, which had maintained the somewhat lazier, more relaxed temporal sensibilities of its eighteenth-century originators. Even though a cricket match could be adjusted to allow for time restraints, the long periods of idleness in which many players were neither at bat nor in the field were an integral part of

The Ted Williams swing.

even a shortened form of the game. Baseball, because it allowed for a more constant exchange between offence and defence, could be played in a couple of hours to everyone's satisfaction. There were, of course, difficulties with the public's newfound infatuation. Shoemaking, for instance, which required that four craftsmen—the burner, laster, healer, and finisher—be present, was often disrupted by one person's absence. Everyone had to be sent home and as often as not that meant a quick sidetrip to play baseball, usually with the miraculously recovered absentee.

Taylor's methods of scientific management eventually extended to the game itself. Very early on, a statistical record of virtually all on-field activities was compiled. The basis for such tabulation is the box score, which first appeared in the *New York Herald* on October 25, 1845, and closely paralleled the style adopted by cricket. It read as follows:

Base Ball Play. —The subjoined in the result of the return match between the New York Base Ball Club and the Brooklyn players, which came off on the ground of the Brooklyn Star Cricket Club yesterday. Messrs Johnson, Wheaton and Van Nostrand were the umpires.

NEW YORK BALL CLUB			BROOKLYN CLUB.		
	Hands Out.	Runs.		Hands Out.	Runs.
Davis.......	2	4	Hunt.........	1	3
Murphy...	0	6	Hines........	2	2
Vail..........	2	4	Gilmore....	3	2
Kline.........	1	4	Hardy.......	2	2
Miller........	2	5	Sharp........	2	2
Case..........	2	4	Meyers.....	0	3
Tucker......	2	4	Whaley.....	2	2
Winslow...	1	6	Forman.....	1	3
	12	37		12[*sic*]	19

To an extent, baseball's statistical heritage is reflected in its one-on-one confrontations of batter versus pitcher, batter versus fielder, runner versus pitcher, and so on. The earliest box scores and statistics, derived from cricket, had to be adapted to accommodate baseball's unique sequential character whereby hits, bases on balls, errors, and clutch hitting accumulate to bring across a run. Generally poorer defensive play (gloves weren't in use) and restrictions on a pitcher's delivery meant that, as in children's baseball today, a batter who made base had an excellent opportunity to

score. Thus, as late as 1868, the batting title was awarded to the player with the greatest average of runs per game.

Henry Chadwick introduced the concept of hits per game and, by 1874, the Boston press were reporting hits per at-bat; by 1876, at-bats had become the official means of tallying batting averages.

As well, with the improvement in fielding and the gradual unshackling of the pitcher when curve pitches and recorded balls and strikes were instituted, some record of pitching achievement became meaningful. The number of pitching categories in 1876 was eleven, including earned-run average and hits allowed. Strikeouts were not officially recorded until 1887.

Achievements in fielding have received the least attention in statistical analyses. The 1876 total of six recorded categories remained unchanged for one hundred years. Of all areas, however, fielding has shown the most marked improvement. As John Thorn and Pete Palmer relate in their study *The Hidden Game of Baseball*, "In 1876...the National League scored 3,066 runs of which only 1,201—39.2 per cent—were earned. By the early 1890s this figure reached 70 per cent, an extraordinary advance. It took until 1920 to reach 80 per cent, and by the late 1940s it leveled off in the 87–89 per cent range, where it remains."

Despite its weaknesses, however, the box score remains baseball's most constant means of keeping tabs on the action on the field. Then, as now, scouts could check which batters were hot and which were not, whether a cagey veteran still had it or whether the ten or eleven hits he previously scattered over nine innings for little damage were now coming in clumps in the early innings, whether a maturing pitching star was now sacrificing strikeouts for a more liberal dose of fielding outs, and whether a moody left fielder's errors were bringing closer the day when he would become a permanent designated hitter. And if this information did not suffice, there was always the official scorer's tabulation, which any fan could freely keep while sitting in the ballpark or listening to the radio.

On August 25, 1877, Buffalo's independent professional team hosted the Canadian Champion London Tecumsehs. Buffalo accumulated fourteen errors to London's nine, while the respective hit totals of five and eleven proved the wisdom of what modern little-league coaches yell to their juvenile batters: "Put the ball in play, anything can happen." So unusual were strikeouts (in winning forty-seven games in 1876, Al Spalding struck out only thirty-nine batters) that only Larry Corcoran (misspelled on the official sheet as "Cocran") was fanned by rival Fred Goldsmith. At the bottom of the official sheet for the game, the number of called strikes was noted as twenty-eight to twenty-one, though it is unclear whether these were for or against. Not surprisingly, the most putouts were registered by first basemen: Frank Heifer of Buffalo, thirteen, and Joe Hornung of London, nine. Catcher Ed McGlynn of Buffalo led all players with six errors, of which five were recorded as passed balls. Both teams surpassed the standard of the day, which saw 6.5 runs scored for every 10 hits (today's ratio is roughly 4 to 10). Finally, London stranded five while scoring nine and Buffalo left six while bringing in four, indicative in some small way that once on base, a runner had a pretty good chance of scoring.

Some 108 years later, a UPI score sheet for a June 20, 1985, game in Toronto between the Blue Jays and the Boston Red Sox reveals two essential changes in baseball over the last century: it was a night game, while all games in 1877 were played in daylight, and the home team was scheduled to bat last, while a hundred years before, teams would decide such matters only on game day.

The 1877 game was not a league match since Buffalo was not a member of the International Association. Touring, tournament, and exhibition games, however, were of far greater significance in the nineteenth century and, unlike today, when only one or two such games might be played in an entire regular season, they dominated the schedules of teams in the 1870s.

In 1985, Toronto returned home for the June 20 game from a devastating road trip that included four losses in Boston. The Blue Jays held a scant 2 1/2 game lead over Detroit and 3 1/2 over the Red Sox. Boston raced to a 5–1 lead after 4 1/2 innings. But in the bottom of the inning, Garth Iorg doubled with one out and Tony Fernandez tripled to bring in a run and scored on Damaso Garcia's single. When Blue Jay pitcher Doyle Alexander got into trouble in the seventh, he was replaced by Jim Acker. Acker induced Jim Rice to hit into an inning-ending double play. In the bottom of the inning, Buck Martinez led off with a single and was replaced by pinch runner Lou Thornton. Garth Iorg picked up his third hit of the game and Fernandez sacrificed the runners to second and third. At that point, starting pitcher Bob Ojeda left the game to be replaced by Bob Stanley. Garcia greeted him with a triple and then Moseby lofted a shallow 150-foot sacrifice fly to centre fielder Steve Lyons. Garcia took off and beat the throw a few feet up the first base line. Gary Lavelle and then Bill Caudill, who recorded his eleventh save of the season, relieved for Toronto.

While it is dangerous to compare games played more than one hundred years apart, several points are worthy of note. Toronto and Boston pitchers combined for seven strikeouts, a fair representation for a modern game, and there were no errors (again not an unusual circumstance). Toronto used four pitchers to Boston's two as opposed to 1877, when one man generally carried the entire load for each team (between 1876 and 1904, pitchers completed over 90 per cent of games started; by 1982, the rate had fallen below 23 per cent). Boston's starting lineup, including the designated hitter (introduced in 1973 after nine teams failed to draw one million fans in 1972), remained intact while Toronto sent out twelve players in addition to its pitchers. In 1877, such switches were not allowed.

Although the official record of the 1985 game is far more revealing of actual moment-by-moment episodes than that of the 1877 match, both demonstrate the tremendous amount of information that baseball collects from every game played. Recording, digesting, and making sense of this information has been a constant challenge to baseball strategists.

Data and observation, the stuff of the scientific method, were brought to bear in the game at an early stage. Science is usually interested in repeated

Crossing home plate was a common experience for the "Say Hey" Kid, Willie Mays. No day of his topped April 30, 1961, when Mays hit four home runs in one game (San Diego Union/Tribune).

testing to validate existing theories. According to theorist Thomas Kuhn, this approach breaks down when more and more anomalies challenge an existing paradigm. The last three decades of the nineteenth century dramatically demonstrated this problem in baseball. We can best imagine the style of play of pre–Civil War ballplayers by watching ten- and eleven-year-olds at play. Skills are mixed: a ten-year-old pitcher suddenly runs to cover first on a sharp ground ball to his first baseman and makes a major-league putout; on the next play, he drops an easy pop fly. And so it was for the adult players of the last century. With professionalism creeping in by the 1860s, however, standardization of the game and its greater predictability meant that old forms of play or rules that did not conform were jettisoned. Today, as skills improve, players naturally adapt to the strategies and rules already in place. In the last century, these rules and strategies had to be invented.

Joe Start, a National League first baseman from 1876 to 1886, is credited by historian David Voigt with introducing the practice of first basemen playing off the unoccupied bag in order to field balls that would formerly have become base hits. The earliest lithographs depicting baseball games reveal that at one time all fielding basemen stuck close to their bag, and though this seems peculiar to us now, a study of baseball in Russia in 1988 showed the second baseman still holding the runner on second, thus leaving a huge hole in the right side of the infield.

Where, at one time, league games might be spaced out to a couple a week, the expanding schedule in the 1880s caused Chicago manager Cap Anson to experiment with a pitching rotation that alternated two former rivals in Buffalo and London, fastball pitcher Larry Corcoran and curve-baller Fred Goldsmith.

Beginning in 1881, the more leisurely cricketing policy that allowed a manager to improvise his batting lineup in the first few innings was changed to require that the team's order be drawn up in advance. Cap Anson could no longer insert himself in the lineup at a point where his team had men on base.

By the 1880s, fielders were backing each other up, learning to recognize the cut-off man (a lesson some have not learned to this day) and shifting their defence depending on the hitter or moving the defence in to cut off a run.

Willie Keeler actually played thirty games at third, shortstop, and second base in 1892 and 1893 despite his left-handedness. Baseball, in deference to the greater number of right-handers in the world, is a counter-clockwise sport though some diagrams of early rounders show that the bases ran in a clockwise fashion. The difficulty for a left-hander on the left side of a counterclockwise diamond is obvious. He would have to field the ball, then turn his body and finally throw. In a game decided by split-second plays at first, there was not time for such fancy footwork. With the exception of the pitcher, the natural right-hander to this day dominates all positions, though the natural southpaw is equally at home at first or in the outfield. Also coveted is the player who uses the throw-right/bat-left combination, not only because he can play all positions but also because, as a left-handed batter, he will have certain advantages over the majority of right-handed pitchers. Switch-hitting, right-handed throwers are next in popularity though their limited ambidexterity is usually purchased at the cost of a somewhat weaker batting average from the left side.

The science of platooning, successfully used by Baltimore Oriole manager Ned Hanlon in the 1890s, is based on the statistical observation that hitters usually do better against a pitcher who throws from the side opposite their hitting. In other words, southpaw Jimmy Key's curve to right-handed batter Dave Winfield starts outside and moves into his strike zone. Winfield gets both a longer look at the ball and the advantage of hitting a ball that is moving into his strength. Left-handed batter Don Mattingly, on the other hand, may be momentarily frozen by the same pitch because it appears that it is going to hit him. This pitch, even if it crosses the strike zone, is moving away from Mattingly's bat. At the major-league level, most players learn to compensate for these disadvantages and to diminish their significance but, on average, a slight variation between the success of right- and left-handed batters will remain. Enough of a variation, in short, to challenge the manager's decision-making power.

Jimmy Key, Toronto Blue Jays' southpaw.

By the last two decades of the nineteenth century, the game's sophistication was such that Fred Pfeffer released in 1889 a book simply titled *Scientific Ball*. A style of play had developed known as "inside baseball". Debates flared throughout the 1880s as to whether it was really possible for a batter to place a hit. Proof that it could be done was accorded by the legendary Baltimore Orioles of the 1890s. The Orioles mastered the hit-and-run play that several teams had tried a decade earlier. With a runner on first, the batter signals for him to take off on the pitch. The hitter's job is to drive the ball behind the runner, towards right field, allowing him to race to third. With a fast runner on first, the batter may opt to take the pitch in a variation known as the run-and-hit on the assumption that the

Lithos of John Montgomery Ward, from The New York Clipper, *Sept. 6, 1879, and A.G. Spalding from* The New York Clipper, *Nov. 22, 1879.*

runner is fast enough to steal second—a play that involves much second-guessing. A slow runner on first often means that the batter will have to take a poke at the ball. If the hit is to a fielder, it is less likely that a double play will occur. The catcher may anticipate such a play and call for a pitch out (a deliberate throwing of the ball outside the strike zone) to improve his chances of throwing out the runner at second. Such a call is less likely, however, if the pitcher is behind in the count, with perhaps no strikes and one or two balls. Such counts lend themselves to stolen bases. Trailing by more than one run late in the game may make a team more reluctant to adopt such strategies, since one additional out would bring the close of the game nearer to hand.

The bunt was also introduced in the nineteenth century but was looked down on, at first, as a somewhat sissy move. Its value in advancing runners or catching the defence playing back on the infield was soon recognized. John Montgomery Ward, who toured the world with A.G. Spalding in 1888–89 and led the players' revolt, which resulted in their forming an independent league in 1890, mastered the bunt as manager of Brooklyn in 1891. A bat made of soft willow was used especially for this purpose and, to confuse the opposition, looked identical to the usual hardwood bat.

No two items have been more often the focus of scientific debate over the past few years than the bat and ball. Early bats were pole-like appendages that players customized only by sawing off the end. In 1884, John Hillerich, owner of a wood-turning business in Louisville, made a custom-ordered bat for Pete Browning; in time, this company became famous as the maker of the Louisville Slugger.

The first bats were flat-sided cricket bats, a style not completely forbidden until 1893. Today's bat must be 2 3/4" in diameter and not more than

42" long, formed from one piece of solid wood (usually ash) or a block of bonded woods in which the grain direction of all pieces is essentially parallel to the bat's length. The modern bat tapers to a thinner handle and generally weighs just over 30 ounces, a far cry from Babe Ruth's 54-ounce model.

Regulating bat construction has not stopped many players from seeking what is perceived to be an unfair advantage. Nothing demonstrates this better than the recent controversy over cork in the bat. When Amos Otis retired from the Kansas City Royals after the 1984 season, he attributed his 193 career home runs to his special hollowed-out cork-filled bats. Batters believe that cork creates a springier, home-run-producing bat, and such superstition persists despite evidence showing that cork only makes the bat lighter, allowing the batter to swing later and with greater speed. Selecting a lighter bat would have the same result as using a cork core, Peter Brancazio, a Brooklyn College physics professor, suggests. A smaller bat, however, also has a smaller striking surface, and given that a 90-mile-per-hour fastball reaches home plate just 0.41 seconds after leaving the pitcher's hand, batters conclude they need all the help they can get. A corked bat provides greater speed rather than the improved loft imputed to it and has a broader surface with which to make contact.

Successful batting is based not only on physiology and choosing the right weapon but on attention to learned habit. The speed of the pitch, which would obviously overwhelm the average fan, is no impediment to the professional. What confounds the batter is, however, what physicists call "the angular velocity" of the ball, which they claim reaches 1,000 degrees as it crosses the plate. It is a bit like a driver viewing a grove of trees in the distance: from afar, he can pick out the trees' individual character, but up close, they become a blur. Since even the major leaguer's gaze velocity is something like 150 degrees per second, it is clear that the much-vaunted skill of some to actually watch the ball connect with the bat and tear off into space is a myth. Since professional hitters make contact on eight out of ten swings (though most often fouling-off the ball), it is obvious that something more than good vision is required. This is where learning plays a role. A batter could choose to watch the ball leave the pitcher's hand and then refocus on the area over the plate. In so doing, he would at least see its location as a blur. He would not have time to hit it, of course, but he would have learned enough from the pitcher's release and the relative location of the ball to guess its movement pattern another time. Generally, the better hitters are those who have done their homework and have the ability to predict the ball's likely destination and speed. To be successful, a batter must have a clear view of the pitcher, keeping his head as steady as possible and his eyes level.

Even after all that, however, many hitters maintain the belief that they can count the number of seams on the ball in flight, and even read the league president's name on it.

Magic properties are also accorded to the ball. A most gifted pitcher, notorious for such beliefs, was the wonderful, eccentric Mark Fidrych. His dazzling 1976 season with Detroit, in which he won nineteen games, was marked by apparent soliloquies on the mound. Actually he was often in dialogue with the ball regarding its future path.

The ball is a sphere of yarn wound around a small core of cork, rubber, or similar material and covered with two strips of cowhide (prior to 1974 horsehide was used) held together by 108 hand-sewn, raised stitches. The ball weighs between 5 and 5 1/4 ounces and measures between 9 and 9 1/4 inches in circumference. Balls are unwrapped, treated with a special

Despite a .324 batting average in the 1919 World Series and professed innocence, Buck Weaver was banished from baseball for having known that several teammates were consorting with gamblers.

mud to dull their white surface, and put into play by the umpire.

While ball measurements had been standardized in 1872, the Ryan dead ball was not ruled official until 1875. Previously, some teams had used red balls while others preferred the solid, one-piece billiard-type ball to the double-covered ball introduced in 1873. When Albert Spalding was granted the National League monopoly, one might have thought that the controversy would be over. It wasn't! As fielding and hitting skills improved over the years, the sluggish dead ball in use in the American League before 1920 and the National before 1921 seemed anomalous. After the First World War, the leagues introduced the more lively rabbit ball, which intensified the game's offence. Later, in light of the action of several members of the Chicago White Sox in throwing the 1919 World Series (which was only revealed towards the end of the 1920 season), the change was rationalized, after the fact, as a means of generating renewed interest in a tarnished game. With the new ball, Babe Ruth (a.k.a. the Sultan of Swat, the Bambino, the Colossus of Clout) hit twenty-five more home runs in 1920 as a New York Yankee (having been traded from the Boston Red Sox in the off season) than in the previous year, for a record-breaking total of fifty-four, which he subsequently bettered with fifty-nine a year later and sixty in 1927.

The postwar period also saw the banning of the spitball, except for those pitchers who were already known practitioners (one of these, Clarence Mitchell of Brooklyn, had the dubious distinction in the 1920 World Series of hitting into a double play and triple play in the same game). This seemed to be yet another blow to pitchers, who had seen the pitching mound retreat from 45 to 50 feet in 1881 and finally to 60 feet 6 inches in 1893, when Amos Rusie's fastballs were deemed too hard to hit at the shorter distance. As well, by the 1880s, umpires were using more than the one or two scuffed and dirty balls that were often intended to last an entire game. Not until 1920, however, when Ray Chapman was and killed by a ball acknowledged to be so dirty as to be invisible, was an effort made to keep a clean, fresh ball in play at all times.

To compensate for the standardization of the ball, pitchers learned new deliveries and in some cases simply cheated. The most common methods included cutting, scuffing, or applying a foreign substance like spit or K-Y Jelly to the ball. In 1987, television cameras revealed in slow motion how Minnesota Twins pitcher Joe Niekro flipped an emery board out of his back pocket while umpires closed in for a closer inspection that would eventually result in his ten-game suspension. A blemish on the surface of the ball disrupts the airflow around it, causing the ball to change course. A similar principle underlies the legal knuckleball, which is thrown with little or no spin by pushing the ball off the fingertips and letting the stitches on it flutter it over the crucial 5 1/2 feet in front of the plate, making it hard for the batter to see.

(The spitball and its brother in arms, the scuffball, have produced some of the game's more bizarre moments. In 1905, the Board of Health in Woodstock, Ontario, banned the spitball, claiming it might spread tuberculosis. In another instance, before the ban, to prevent Chicago's Ed Walsh from blatantly licking the ball, opponents would smear it with horse manure.)

Scientific understanding changed the nature of how baseball was played in the nineteenth century and the game remained essentially the same in the twentieth—spitballs, rabbit balls, and designated hitters notwithstanding. It may indeed be that baseball's decline in the 1960s was caused not only by pro football's rise but also by baseball's apparent predictability. If so, then one of the things that helped bring it back into favour in the 1970s and 1980s was a return of the good old scientific spirit.

In the 1920s, such reporters as Hugh Fullerton had constructed apparently sophisticated models used to predict the outcome of pennant races, but such methods of analysis being less than scientific, they fell back on their able though by no means exact impressions. "In my plan," Fullerton wrote, "the pitcher is 36 percent of the defensive strength, catcher 14, first baseman 8, second baseman 9, third baseman 5 1/2, and so around the field." At that point, Fullerton's explanation ceases, but by awarding Washington 11,745 offensive and defensive points, he had them narrowly beating New York and Philadelphia for the American League pennant. In the National League, Chicago's 11,460 points edged them ahead of St. Louis and Pittsburgh. In fact, St. Louis narrowly beat out the Cubs while Washington disappointed their fans, finishing fifth. Philadelphia and the Yankees were 1–2. Not a bad prediction, but somewhat suspect in its methodology.

Earnshaw Cook's *Percentage Baseball*, released in 1964, was a predecessor of the type of analysis popularized by statisticianBill James. Cook's scoring index broadened the measure of the batter's performance by incorporating hits, stolen bases, walks, and so on, and he developed fundamental scoring equations based on 75,000 actual situations. He concluded among other things that teams should never sacrifice, hitters should bat in order of excellence, platooning should be avoided, and pitchers (even the starter) should be used for only two or three innings, much as if they were all relievers. Cook suggested that a second-division team following his recipe would improve by 250 runs and could make a run for the pennant.

Cook's conclusions took little account of extraordinary game situations or players. Would it really make sense, for instance, consistently to bat Babe Ruth first in the lineup where he would be guaranteed at least 162 at-bats a season with no one on base? Would one really take Bob Gibson out of a game after three no-hit innings? And forgoing the sacrifice bunt as part of a team's attack simply removes an element of surprise and allows the infielders to play farther back.

In fairness to Cook, he was working in an era of few other statistical critics. In those days before powerful desk-top computers, his reliance on an electric calculator entitled him to some rather outrageous conclusions.

With the formation of the Society for American Baseball Research in 1971, a new breed of analyst emerged. These fan-researchers from outside the baseball establishment expanded Cook's groundwork and did it within the context of relativity. Bill James took his part-time statistical fascination and turned it into an analytical growth industry. James not only crunched numbers but, by studying present context and history, arrived at clever and often humorous parables of the modern game.

One of those dealt with the mysteries of the stolen base. James concluded that it is not very important. Certainly there were a lot of stolen bases in Ty Cobb's era, but at that time the game was characterized by a dead ball that is no longer used. Scratching for a lone run by means of singles, sacrifices, hit-and-runs, and stolen bases became less meaningful with the advent of the live-ball, home-run era in the 1920s. "In the old days," John McGraw observed, "the steal of second base or the taking of an extra base on a short hit often meant the one run needed to win. With the batters able to smack the ball at will, what is the use of running the risk of having men thrown out on daring chances? They might better stand still and score on a long hit." By the 1950s, catchers were often squat, power-hitting behemoths, such as Smokey Burgess, Stan Lopata, or Frank House, who could no more toss out a Rickey Henderson than dance *Swan Lake*. The return of the stolen base in the 1960s was a response to ill-equipped defences and the influx of black and Hispanic players for whom the stolen base was a part of their earliest training.

On artificial surfaces the defence must respond more quickly to ground balls. Fleet shortstops, such as Tony Fernandez of the Toronto Blue Jays, are a prized commodity.

The construction of larger ballparks in the late 1960s, which cut down on home-run production, and the introduction of artificial surfaces helped Lou Brock set a stolen-base record of 118 in 1974.

James, however, critiqued the stolen base as little more than fancy window dressing and of far less significance than the categories for doubles and triples. Pete Palmer, a fellow sabermetrician, supported James's theory with statistics showing that with a runner on first and none out, teams scored .783 runs. An unsuccessful stolen-base attempt drops that to .249, whereas a successful steal raised the scoring total to 1.068. In other words, success raises the run total by less than .3 while failure drops it by .5. Home runs and stolen bases are competing methods of advancing base runners, James concluded, and because the risk of the attempted steal outweighs the advantages to be gained by staying put, stolen bases are of strategic use only to a team that lacks power.

James, however, is the first to acknowledge that his findings, like those of a true scientist, remain subject to re-evaluation and change. Nothing, even a baseball statistic, is absolute. Yet for all the appearance of tossing us back into an ocean of indeterminacy, the game remains surprisingly mature. The attempt to create a science of baseball often leads to more questions than answers and causes some to revert to the more ideal territory of magic.

Yogi Berra may not have been the first to observe that baseball is 90 per cent mental while the other half remains physical; he just stated the equation in a way that made perfect sense in every way but the mathematical.

BALLPARKS

"Is there anything that can tell more about an American summer," Thomas Wolfe wrote in 1938, "than, say, the smell of the wooden bleachers in a small town baseball park, that resinous, sultry and exciting smell of old, dry wood?" It matters not the score, nor the teams.

The ballpark is the arena in which the public expresses, through its support of the home team, a sense of urban and regional solidarity in the face of a diverse and potentially alienating environment. The ability of the modern baseball team to create a sense of civic identity for large metropolitan and regional territories demonstrates the successful transition of the sport from its nineteenth-century origins as a more narrowly defined local entity.

Possibly this identity explains why the old parks, such as Fenway and Tiger, tug so strongly on a baseball fan's emotions. By offering a collective history of a people's sense of place, ballparks have in their own way come to symbolize life in the towns where they are located.

It is tempting to view ballpark change as an evolutionary advance from the simple to the complex; however, the only real advance has in fact been to shift the ballpark out of the urban texture of which it is a part and allow it to stand alone as a kind of icon for civic progress.

Baseball's predecessor in North America was known as townball largely because its play evolved to suit the peculiarities of local space. With no outfield fence, the long drive was pointless if the outfielders were positioned properly. And because the ball was softer before the practice of hitting the runner with the ball was abolished, most of the action was centred within the diamond. Thus, townball was similar to contemporary children's games in that the players least likely to catch a towering fly are placed in the outfield on the understanding that the ball will never be hit there anyway.

The earliest parks were not unlike the countless small-town and open-field diamonds in use by amateurs today. The Knickerbockers' ball field in Hoboken was an empty grass lot, which, lacking the swath of infield dirt created for later natural-grass parks, resembled in appearance if not texture the modern artificial surface. One nineteenth-century observer, Seymour Church, described it as "a perfect greensward almost the year around. Nature must have foreseen the needs of baseball and destined the place especially for that purpose."

In another sense, early baseball fields anticipated the uniformity of modern stadiums. Lacking short porches, such as Fenway's 315-foot

Opposite: Commercial advertisements on outfield fences, a fixture in old ballparks, have been replaced by team logos in the new stadiums.

(down the line) distance to the "Green Monster" in left, the earliest grounds, following Cartwright's codification of the rules, played little part in creating different interpretations of the game. A 275-foot fly ball, whether in the wide-open Elysian Fields in 1846 or in Pittsburgh's Three Rivers Stadium in 1989, is just a medium distance out, since the Pittsburgh stadium satisfies rule 1.04 in the Official Baseball Rules, which states that "Any playing field constructed by a professional club after June 1, 1958, shall provide a minimum distance of 325 feet from home base to the nearest fence, stand or other obstruction on the right or left field foul lines, and a minimum distance of 400 feet to the center field fence." Between the Elysian Fields and Three Rivers Stadium, however, are poised the grand old parks of baseball, such as the Polo Grounds with its 258-foot distance from home plate to the right-field foul pole, over which Dusty Rhodes just barely hit the home runs that helped win the 1954 World Series for the New York Giants.

The first era of playing fields required little more than four markers and a level, relatively harmless playing surface. Even in the biggest cities in those days, the civilizing dictum persisted that a person should be able to walk into the countryside within fifteen minutes. Open spaces with shading trees were maintained. In that sense, the ball diamonds of the mid-nineteenth century were not much different from the fields on which the Berbers of North Africa had played for thousands of years. Games had something of the relaxed air of cricket or croquet. A tent might be set up for spectators in the more competitive games, but they generally lounged in the available natural shade. The top-hatted umpire standing along the first-base side looked like one of the crowd. On the other side of the plate, a scorekeeper might have sat at a big table with a pencil and a large book.

The construction in 1862 of an enclosed ballpark in New York by William Cammeyer was one of the most significant developments in the history of bat-and-ball games.

The first enclosed park had been a race track, New York's Fashion Race Course, where 1,500 spectators had paid fifty cents to watch the 1858 championship series. Four years later, Cammeyer opened the Union Grounds on the former site of a skating rink at Lee Avenue and Rutledge Street in Brooklyn. Cammeyer provided ball teams with a playing ground but kept the ten-cent entry fee per spectator. The 1,500 seats were nothing more than benches, primarily for women spectators, with several club-houses for the teams. Most male fans, as in the days of the open-field games, stood around on the edge of the play.

The steady growth of professionalism in the 1860s, particularly after the Civil War, meant that teams were no longer willing to strike profitless bargains with entrepreneurs like Cammeyer. In Brooklyn, the Capitoline Grounds attracted the city's most powerful club, the Atlantics. For his part, Cammeyer struck a deal with the New York Mutuals, a team originally organized by volunteer firemen in a New York company of that name. Dependent as they were on city hall for favours, they soon came under the influence of William Marcy (Boss) Tweed, the corrupt foreman of the Tammany Hall machine that ran New York's civic affairs. (The coroner's office had a particular preference for hiring ballplayers.) The Mutuals moved to Union Grounds, now expanded to 6,000 seats, and eventually entered the National Association, with Cammeyer as president in 1871 (the year of Tweed's downfall). Unable to retain all gate receipts for himself, Cammeyer had settled for the next-best thing—becoming a club owner. The players, who had once controlled a team's affairs, were now labourers subject to the necessity of negotiating a salary.

A higher level of competition in which results were less predictable led

Open-field play from a game on St. Helen's Island in Montreal in the 1870s.

Baseball at Wesley Park, Winnipeg, 1920. Early enclosed ballparks had generous out-field dimensions.

to players' being paid as a method of retaining their loyalty.

Entrepreneurs from small town to big city built ballparks to broadcast their civic pride to the world. Such teams as the Philadelphia Athletics, who got their start in 1859 among the amateur singers of the Handel and Hayden Society, were soon taken over by more overt political connections. Their elephant logo, still worn by the transplanted Oakland Athletics, reflected their association with the Republican party in the nineteenth century. Political organizations sponsored baseball teams for the same reasons beer companies do—to advertise their product.

While a new formality ruled the wooden ballparks in which high-level baseball was played, the nature of the game did not change radically. Land was plentiful and inexpensive and the great distance to the outfield wall meant that play was not greatly constrained by the park's perimeter. But the fans were still able to crowd about the field and this was to play a significant role in ending the grand winning streak of the Cincinnati Red Stockings. Having gone undefeated the year before, they won their first twenty-seven games in 1870 but, playing in the Capitoline Grounds against the Brooklyn Atlantics, they finished nine innings tied 5–5. Finally in the eleventh, they took the lead, but Brooklyn's at-bat was aided by a fan who jumped on Cal McVey's back as he attempted to field a ball, and the Atlantics won 8–7.

One of the hundreds of ballparks built in this era was that of the London Tecumsehs of the International Association in 1877. The association was the first serious rival to the National League, formed one year previously. Its teams were generally from smaller urban areas, though Pittsburgh was also represented. In April, the managers of the Tecumsehs succeeded in procuring suitable grounds on the outskirts of town. It was reported that "The citizens of London, at least the thousands of them who took a deep interest in baseball, could not thank the small souled alderman or their equally tightlaced ward politicians for their actions in compelling the Tecumsehs to purchase playing grounds outside city limits but no other course was open to them." They leased five to six acres in Kensington, north of a bridge, where it was intended that operation commence at once and that the grounds would be in suitable trim before the month was out.

Stands were to be erected at the southwest and northwest corners, with seating for 600 in the covered grandstand and considerably more in general admission. The Tecumsehs were congratulated for securing excellent grounds within reasonable distance of the city.

The Grand Pavilion of the South End Grounds in Boston (burned to the ground in 1894).

The grandstand was used as a dressing room for the players, and the upstairs was reserved for the press. The Montreal and Dominion Telegraph companies strung wires to the grounds. The infield was sodded, rolled, and levelled and was as smooth as a billiard table, while the outfield was scraped and holes were filled up. The baselines, about three feet wide, were filled with hard clay and rolled with a heavy iron roller. A force pump was erected in the grounds near the public stands to dispense ice-cold water during the hot days of summer.

The nearby Great Western and Grand Trunk offered baseball fans in Port Stanley, St. Thomas, Exeter, and Strathroy discounts for round-trip tickets. On the May 24 holiday more than 8,000 fans paid twenty-five cents each to watch London lose a dramatic ten-inning encounter 7–6 to the eventual National League champions from Boston.

The transitory nature and variance in size of ballparks of the era were most evident in Boston's several playing fields. One of these, South End Grounds, went by a number of different names (Walpole Street Grounds, Union Baseball Grounds, Grand Pavilion) from 1871 (the first season of the National Association Boston Red Stockings) until the Boston Braves departed in August 1914. An elegantly double-decked grandstand with twin spires towering overhead had to be rebuilt after a May 15, 1894, fire that started in the bottom of the third inning of a Boston–Baltimore game and completely destroyed the original building. The rebuilt park was bounded on its left-field side by railroad tracks, and its foul pole was only 250 feet from home plate. Right field, bounded by Columbus Avenue, was only 255 feet from the foul pole. Left-centre field drifted off to 450 feet, but the general outfield distance was 440 feet.

Plans for Cincinnati's new grounds, announced in 1884, revealed the future direction of ballpark design. The first-base side of the uncovered pavilion was bounded by Western Avenue and the third-base side by Findlay Street. There was seating for 6,500 and a decidedly modern touch in the inclusion of twelve private boxes. On opening day, however, the stands collapsed, killing one fan and injuring several others.

While vast dimensions characterized most of these parks, there were significant exceptions. These foretold a future in which land values and adjoining land use would curtail the grand visions of team owners.

In 1883, the regular players of Chicago's National League White Stockings hit 13 home runs. A year later, the total climbed to 134 before falling back to 55 in 1885. The rest of the league did not join in on Chicago's 1884 batting binge: the pennant winners, Providence, hit 21 homers that year and only one player other than a White Stocking hit in the double figures. Dan Brouthers of Buffalo hit 14 but it placed him fifth in the league behind Chicago's Ed Williamson (27), Fred Pfeffer (25), Abner Dalrymple (22), and Cap Anson (21).

Forbes Field, home of the Pittsburgh Pirates from June 30, 1909, to June 18, 1970, and to the Homestead Grays from 1939 to 1948.

Perhaps the only way to explain this situation is to look at Chicago's home park. Lake Front Park, a wooden structure on the grounds of a former park bounded by Michigan Avenue, Washington Street, the Illinois Central Railroad tracks, and Randolph Street, was one of the tiniest parks then in use. The White Stockings occupied it from May 5, 1883, to the end of 1884. Their 1883 statistics suggest that at first they relied on the more cautious line-drive style of hitting of the day. By the next season, however, they began to take deadly aim at outfield fences only 180 feet down the left-field line, 280 to left centre, 300 to centre, 252 to right centre, and 196 to the right-field foul pole.

In a game on May 30, Williamson hit three home runs, and in early August, Anson hit five in a two-game span. Such hitting had never been seen before, but because Chicago finished fourth, the significance of their achievement was overlooked. It would take a future generation to demonstrate the value of the long ball, both for winning games and drawing fans.

If nothing else, the places of this era had a quaint character. Hilltop

Park, home of the New York Highlanders (predecessors of the Yankees), in the first decade of the twentieth century was located at 168th Street and Broadway. It seated only 15,000 fans, but from the height of the stands one could see down the Hudson River. A Durham Bull tobacco sign in right centre, more than 500 feet from home plate, was shaped like a bull and towered over the field at twice the height of the rest of the fence.

All parks of this age were built for function rather than longevity. Even dressing rooms were sometimes neglected, forcing players to parade to the ballpark in open carriages with their bats in a little bag slung over the shoulder. As in Boston, fire destroyed most of these places. When Louisville's park burned in 1899, the team moved to Pittsburgh to become the Pirates. In other cases, ballparks were doomed by baseball's precarious status in the community. In 1889, the Giants had to leave their old grounds when the city announced the extension of 111th Street through centre field. The team eventually settled on its Polo Grounds site at 8th Avenue and 155th Street.

To guarantee some permanence and increase seating capacity, owners of ball clubs began to take a greater interest in stadium construction. The parks built in this era, culminating in the construction of Yankee Stadium in 1923, were not only among the grandest but are considered by many romantics today to be unmatched by modern parks.

What in large measure distinguishes those parks is that they were built for baseball alone and were often tightly constrained by available inner-city property. They conformed to the urban grid and occupied space in a manner no different from other features of the built streetscape. In the movie *Angels in the Outfield*, characters climbed out of cabs, took a few steps on the sidewalk, opened a door, and were inside Forbes Field. Because these parks were built within tight boundaries, they often contained odd angles, overhanging balconies, and wide-open outfield spaces. The lore of baseball has since been dominated by the adventures made possible by such peculiarities.

Ballparks of this steel-and-concrete era date from the 1909 construction of Shibe Park in Philadelphia and Forbes Field in Pittsburgh. Philadelphia had the first concrete-and-steel stadium in the majors. Shibe Park conformed to the street grid of the city but was truly a transitional park, with its enormous 447-foot distance to dead centre and 390-foot left- and right-centre power alleys. Mel Ott, who hit 511 career home runs for the Giants, never hit a home run in Shibe Park in ten seasons of play there against the Phillies.

Work on Forbes Field commenced on March 1, 1909, and the first game was played on June 30 of that year. Vast steel stands were erected, and right field, which had been a partial hollow, was filled in and levelled. The field stood at the northeast corner of Schenley Park and was tightly bounded by the surrounding Boquet Street along the first-base line and Sinnott Street and the Cathedral of Learning along the third-base line. The park originally seated 24,000 in the triple-decked grandstand, left-field pavilion, and right-field open bleacher. An additional wing at right centre increased seating capacity to over 33,000. A fence was constructed in 1947, reducing the home-run hitting distance into left field by thirty feet (since the idea was to improve Hank Greenberg's home-run chances, the area behind the fence came to be known as Greenberg Gardens). The enclosure stayed after Greenberg's retirement as an inducement to slugger Ralph Kiner. Kiner was traded to the Cubs in 1953, but Branch Rickey's efforts to remove the fence immediately were nixed by the league president, who said it would have to stay until season's end.

The most famous memory of Forbes Field is Bill Mazeroski's historic

Toronto baseball fans in formal turn-of-the-century dress.

home run in the last half of the ninth inning of the 1960 World Series game that gave the Pirates a 4–3 series triumph. In old newsreels, the ball can be seen sailing over the ivy-covered brick wall in left field and disappearing into a grove of trees in Schenley Park, where cows once grazed.

Ebbets Field, opened in 1913 in the Pigtown section of Brooklyn, was served by a system of trolley cars. The skill that spectators had to display in avoiding the vehicles, both here and at the former Washington Park site, eventually gave the team its name of Trolley Dodgers. The right-field playing area was bounded by Bedford Avenue, and outfielder Carl Furillo became an expert at playing the fourteen angles at which a ball came off the twenty-foot wall and the twenty-foot screen above. "Proceed carefully," a writer noted of Carl, "the man's armed."

The trip to Ebbets Field was a grand urban American experience from the moment the train rushed out of the tunnel and emptied into the Prospect Park station. Up the stairs and onto Flatbush Avenue, one was assaulted by honking cars and perhaps the drifting smell from hot-dog stands selling Stahl-Meyer frankfurters. The clock tower of the Bond Bakery building was visible, then the Botanical Garden, and finally in the distance, Ebbets Field. With its cool brick exterior, arched windows, and decorative stonework and its placement at the very edge of the sidewalk, Ebbets was part of its urban texture. Past the turnstiles, one ascended a series of ramps that led to tunnels exiting out to the high-pitched stands themselves. The grass seemed brilliantly green; Gladys Gooding played the organ; and a smell of sweat, tobacco, and peanuts lingered in the air. The Schaefer Beer sign on the right-centre scoreboard, erected after the Second World War, recorded hits and errors, and Abe Stark offered a free suit to any batter who hit his sign.

Braves Field in Boston, situated on a former golf course, opened in August 1915 on a lot measuring 850 feet by 675 feet. Braves owner James Gaffney set the park well back from Commonwealth Avenue near the railway tracks so he could sell the frontage. The park cost one million dollars, used 750 tons of steel, and 8.2 million pounds of cement, and provided seating for 40,000. A ten-foot-high concrete wall surrounded the entire park. Gaffney, an enthusiast of good base running, wanted a playing field large enough to allow inside-the-park home runs in any of the three outfield areas.

Chicago's Wrigley Field remained until the summer of 1988 the only park without lighting for night games. William Wrigley, intent on installing lights as early as 1941, had donated them to America's war effort and it took nearly forty-seven years for the darkness to be lifted. This is only one of the strange twists of fate surrounding this place. Ground-breaking for what was then Weeghman Park at Clark and Addison streets, a busy northside Chicago residential area, took place March 4, 1914, and the first game was played less than two months later, on April 23. Approval to open first had to be obtained from the 1,000 property owners within a three-block radius of the park. The occupants were the Chicago Whales, members of the upstart Federal League, which lasted but two seasons. Charles Weeghman, former owner of the Whales, purchased the National League Cubs and moved them to his new enclosure. The combination of brick with Boston and Bittersweet ivy has always been Wrigley Field's identifying mark. It was within this plantation that Cub left-fielder Andy Pafko lost Roy Cullenbine's (Detroit) hit in the 1945 World Series.

The drier, less resistant air associated with daylight games and the wind that came off Lake Michigan ten blocks away combined to make Wrigley a home-run paradise—as it was in late May 1979 when Philadelphia beat the hometown Cubs 23–22.

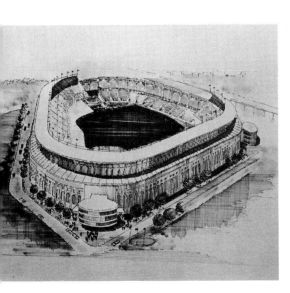

Plans for modernization of Yankee Stadium undertaken after the 1973 season.

Comiskey Park, Chicago; home of the White Sox since 1910.

Of all parks, the Polo Grounds was the oddest, with short foul lines of less than 300 feet, while deepest centre was 475 feet away. In this mammoth space, Willie Mays ran under Vic Wertz's long drive in the 1954 World Series, thus guaranteeing the Giants a first-game victory and eventual series sweep. Even more famous was Bobby Thomson's left-field home run in the 1951 pennant playoff with Brooklyn. If the game had been played in Ebbets Field, the hit would have been an innocent fly out.

Yankee Stadium, with its favourable dimensions in right field, was an inviting target for Babe Ruth's prodigious drives, while the Yankees could load up with southpaws at home, forcing enemy right-handed batters to hit mammoth outs to the alleys in left centre that stretched over 450 feet. Monuments to Ruth, Gehrig, manager Miller Huggins, and president Ed Barrow were erected in centre field, everyone confident that they would not interfere with play. Following renovation of Yankee Stadium in the mid-1970s, the left-centre fence was moved in to 430 feet and the monuments now rest between the old and new walls.

The parks of this era, from the soggy-blanket atmosphere of the Polo Grounds to the crackling autumn sunshine of late September in Fenway or the ivy-covered walls of Wrigley, have provided baseball with the unique settings that have been crucial to the creation of the game's mythology. Their eccentricity and unfairness have been condemned by some, but to many their uniqueness was their most positive feature. Each of these parks required different types of skills. Some favoured righties, others southpaws; some rewarded sluggers, others contact hitters. Lineups had to be juggled, strategy was challenged, the unexpected event became the staple of hot-stove discussion and added to the game's somewhat mythic status as a national pastime. The spectator was rewarded with visual treats: Chicago's Comiskey Park offers a view of city parkland through the wide arches in the outfield stands; on park benches below the stands, wire-mesh fencing at ground level sometimes separates fans from the left-fielder by a matter of inches.

The final element tying these places to their individual city locations was the outfield fence, festooned with advertising for local beer companies, insurance salesmen, and car dealers.

In Toronto's Maple Leaf Stadium, the bare-backed lady on a Sealy mattress in centre field was many a youth's first semi-pornographic experience.

Ironically, though the parks of this era are perceived today as monuments of a golden age, enthusiasm was often a long time coming. For one thing, the new steel and concrete were colder than the old knotty wood, and the larger size of these parks seemed to dwarf the fans and their contribution to the game experience.

The casual informality of older parks was missing. Fans who once lounged in the far extremes of the outfield grass were now removed from the fields to bleacher seats. From seats in the distant reaches of the second deck, the view was unsatisfying. Umpires who once bellowed out substitutions so everyone could hear were replaced in this role by the more impersonal public-address system. Where at one time crowds of 5,000 to 10,000 were considered large, now upwards of 30,000 might pass through modern turnstiles. Fans were ushered in through several entrances and the Boston correspondent for *The Sporting News* criticized this feature of the new Fenway Park: "I find much of the old sociability gone," he wrote. "At the old grounds you were continually running into old friends as the grandstand and bleacher patrons passed through one long runway." Located in newly developed parts of the city, these new parks were sometimes not as accessible as the old ones: Fenway's early low attendance was attributed to the fans' difficulty in adjusting to new travel patterns.

In the old parks, fans could recognize players by their faces, but the huge reaches of Yankee Stadium necessitated the wearing of numbers.

In Brooklyn's Ebbets Field, any ball-player hitting the Abe Stark sign in right field won a suit.

And the players who had once dressed elsewhere and rode in uniform to the park now entered and left the stadium dressing room in the anonymity of civilian mufti.

Even the architectural character we have come to prize, such as Fenway's seventeen different walls, facets, and barriers hugging the contours of available land within a layout that blocked any significant expansion beyond its original limits, was criticized at first for appearing to be cut from a jigsaw puzzle.

Unlike famous men honoured in their generation, many ballparks would be lauded only after they were gone. In many cases, they fell victim to the times. The idea of replacing the past with a veneer of the modern prevailed for several decades after the Second World War. The old ballparks fit the unchanging character of the teams in the major leagues during the first half of the century. By the mid-1950s, many of the old connections were unwinding, culminating in the departure of the Giants and Dodgers from New York following the 1957 season.

In the mid-1950s, Robert Moses, the czar of New York's civic administration, had proposed building a dome stadium in Brooklyn, and Ebbets Field was torn down in 1960 to be replaced by apartment buildings. The Polo Grounds lasted a few more years, serving as home to the expansion New York Mets. Here, in the team's early days, when Roger Craig finally won a game (after eighteen losses) on a last-inning home run, the fans parodied the Bobby Thomson home-run scene of a decade before.

By the end of the 1960s, new parks were being built in Pittsburgh, St. Louis, and Cincinnati. Football was the great sport of the decade, and these new stadiums were multi-purpose. In a sense, they robbed the game of some of its character.

The old parks, their vistas, dimensions, and outfield advertising, were clearly products of a specific city. In a sense, baseball had to conform to the spatial requirements and imagery of its locale. The new parks were a recognition that baseball was part of the entertainment industry, sought by many cities. The game now made demands that at one time would have been scoffed at. Ballparks were now generally built on huge tracts of land, and baseball was now in control of its surroundings. Symmetry reigned, benefiting neither right- nor left-handed players, and around the stadium, the old grid was, whenever necessary, overwhelmed by moatlike parking complexes. Completing the process, the internal fences of the field were altered: local entrepreneurs disappeared and were replaced by individual team logos.

With baseball's increasing value as a small but highly prestigious industry, the close ties it had developed with the cities in which it was played were weakened. Stadium design changed its focus to a fixed idea of what best suited its play. The irony, however, was that the loss of interplay between the particular city and baseball gave the play a kind of homogeneity, sterility, and predictability. In the process, much of the incongruity of the early-twentieth-century parks, which had shaped the oral and playing heritage of the game, was lost.

The loss, however, is fortunately only partial. In New York, Yankee Stadium was renovated rather than abandoned and though left field has moved slightly, the knowledge that this is where Ruth, DiMaggio, and Mantle played remains. Boston, Detroit, and Chicago retain old parks, though in each case there is talk of change. Their survival suggests that the rush to desert other parks of the same vintage in the 1950s and 1960s was premature and ill-advised.

Making sense of ballparks ultimately requires a calculation of the ways in which your team can win as many games as possible at home and still

The SkyDome in downtown Toronto features a retractable roof, allowing the Blue Jays the comfort of sunny day games and no danger of being rained (or snowed) out.

win enough games in the other guys' parks.

Boston has always been a hitter's park, a fact that has seen that team load up on talented sluggers only to watch their demoralized pitching staff lose games that count on the road. Atlanta's Fulton County Stadium and Chicago's Wrigley also favour the hitter, but one looks in vain for World Series victories by any of these teams since Boston last won in 1918 (the Cubs go back to 1908 in pre-Wrigley days, and Atlanta has never made the World Series). Perhaps parks like these lure teams into an empty bravado. At least the Yankees, for all their power, played in the humbling dimensions of their left-centre field. The message of such a place was that you had better store up some pitchers for that rainy day when your hitting shuts down.

Kansas City and St. Louis, two of the most successful clubs of the late 1970s and 1980s, built their offences with speed and pitching, realizing that in the other team's park, any deficiency in attack would be more than compensated for by able defence. St. Louis has a more generous foul territory than many other parks and this adds to the number of pop-fly outs. The Cardinals, playing on an artificial surface, have relied on their speed, pitching, and ability to put the ball in play to counteract an absence of power. With so many artificial-surface parks in the National League, their strategy has been rewarded both at home and away.

Dome stadiums, the most apparently similar of all stadiums, in fact have inconsistencies. The Astrodome is a pitcher's park, which will continue to frustrate generations of Houston long-ball hitters. The Metrodome in Minneapolis and Seattle's Kingdome are both considered ideal hitters' parks and Minnesota has already created its own character by virtue of its noise levels and the "Hefty bag" right-field wall. Chavez Ravine in Los Angeles and Kansas City's Royals Stadium are both modern parks built specifically for baseball and are generally applauded for their single purpose. Toronto's SkyDome will take a few years of play before sound conclusions can be drawn, though there are many, from the Commissioner of Baseball down, who generally welcome the flexibility of such a facility.

If anything, the most harmful development to the entire character of the game, far more devastating than the loss of angles or overhanging balconies, is the replacement of grass by artificial surfaces.

The argument against artificial turf is at once an aesthetic and a functional one. First used in an exhibition series between the visiting Dodgers and Astros (because grass could not be grown in the Astrodome) on March 19, 1966, artificial turf was limited to the infield area. There were complaints, however, about the erratic spin the ball took from the turf to the dirt. By 1970, Cincinnati's Riverfront Stadium had done away with infield dirt, and others quickly followed suit, covering the entire field with a pool-table–like artificial surface with sliding cutouts around the bases. The look and smell of a summer game disappeared. It was a development, however, consistent with attempts to make the game more predictable, more in line with an ideal image of how it should be played—the same philosophy that bred symmetrical parks with no thought to the benefits of unique character.

The irony, of course, is that this attempt to achieve the "ideal" changed the game in ways no one could have foreseen. Weaker hitters who chop the ball had averages boosted. The ground-rule double in the form of a ball bouncing over the outfield fence robbed the game of the excitement of a runner trying to score from first. Outfielders were more reluctant to dive for balls, fearing turf burn (if the Orioles and Mets had played the 1969 World Series on turf, the Miracle Mets might not have won). Bunts become less of a threat because they roll much faster. Outfielders can get away with weaker arms, counting on the ball to skim home if they can get it past second. Infielders rely less on fielding skills and more on a strong arm. Playing farther back, they have to make a longer throw to first. They are rewarded, however, by a truer bounce, which is a friendly way of saying that there is not as much need to play the ball—you simply wait for it to reach the fielder's glove. Learning how to compensate for erratic bounces on real grass makes for better, more resourceful fielders. Turf also cheapens the hitting game. Outfielders stay back because they can run faster; hits that fall in front of them, with the right bounce, can turn into inside-the-park home runs.

Ironically, turf does something that modern baseball design tried to prevent—it benefits one type of team. Chop-hitting, fast teams obviously benefit from turf, and one has no argument with such results. After all, these teams also have to play on grass surfaces.

One can only laugh at the efforts of major-league baseball to remove the quaint peculiarities of individual parks. However, what artificial surfaces do goes beyond lineups. A team that plays mostly on grass suffers on turf because the quicker action of the ball on the artificial surface disrupts timing. A turf team playing on grass suffers in its fielding but is compensated by the ball's more sluggish movement. Basically, we end up with teams playing two different types of games. Parks of the past, regardless of whether they favoured hitters or pitchers, played the same for both teams. Today, that is no longer the case.

Lastly, artificial surfaces have the same potential as the modern, similarly designed parks to rob the game of its unique moments. In the old grass-and-dirt ballparks, field conditions often led to unexpected game outcomes. If a ground ball hit to Fred Lindstrom of the Giants had bounced true in the final game of the 1924 World Series, his opponent, Walter Johnson, would never have won a series with the Washington Senators.

And what about the bouncing ball from the bat of Bill Virdon in the bottom of the eighth in the seventh game of the 1960 World Series, with the Yankees leading the Pirates 7–4. It appeared to be a certain double play. The ball hit something, however, and flew up into Tony Kubek's throat. Everyone was safe, and the Pirates eventually scored five runs in the inning. On artificial turf, such an event is not likely to happen, but there are no guarantees: on September 13, 1979, as the Expos battled the Pirates in a classic pennant race, defeat seemed certain for Montreal when, with the bases loaded and two out in the bottom of the ninth, Rusty Staub hit a lazy bouncer to first. It hit a zipper in the artificial turf, and bounced high off Larry Bittner's glove. Ellis Valentine scored the tying run, and Larry Parrish the winner, as Bittner threw to third rather than home.

In two consecutive games in late 1988, Dave Stieb of the Toronto Blue Jays lost two no-hitters with two out and two strikes on the batter in the ninth inning. In the first game, on Cleveland's grass surface, a bouncing ball hit a rut in the field and bounced crazily over second-baseman Manny Lee's head. One no-hitter lost. Less than a week later, on Toronto's artificial turf, a looping liner fell just beyond first baseman Fred McGriff's glove. On grass, he might have dived and caught the ball. Another no-hitter lost.

For many the complaint about artificial turf is largely a matter of aesthetics: no matter how often the some fans attend games played on turf, nothing can replace the smell of fresh grass and the sight of that marvellous expanse of brown dirt around the field.

North America is probably served by a far greater variety of ballpark types

Buffalo's Pilot Field, home of the Triple A Bisons, is integrated into the city's downtown streetscape and features post-modern, art-deco–type design.

today than at any other time in its history. The few remaining older parks are wonderful models for those who, in the future, might be willing to experiment with the old square-shaped parks and some imbalances in outfield dimensions. It is sometimes argued that to design such imbalance outside the context of an existing, limiting urban grid is a kind of architectural fraud. However, such an argument can be countered with the view that incongruity has the best of all functional purposes—it contributes to the unexpected and the wondrous. If there is a post-modern trend in ballpark construction, its model is Pilot Field in Buffalo. Built to include all the modern amenities and the ability to double in capacity, its design nevertheless was dictated, like that of the old parks, by the existing streetscape.

Pilot Field's features combine many of the elements associated with post-modern architectural design: great tuning-fork columns balance the exterior decorative arches, and the green metal roof is topped by pennant-waving cupolas. These and the Pilot Field balcony overlooking Marine Midland Plaza are deliberately reminiscent of, and tributes to, older ballpark design. Neatly fitted into the urban grid and complementing some of the older structures surrounding it, the park is nevertheless a completely modern place in terms of comfort and function. The horseshoe-shaped stadium design guarantees each fan an ideal vantage point. The innovative food-court area, state-of-the-art irrigation system, and two restaurant patios for watching the game are further refinements. Pilot Field's triumphal blend of old and new corresponds to Charles Jencks's definition of post-modernism as "double coding: the combination of modern techniques with something else (usually traditional building) in order for architecture to communicate with the public and a concerned minority, usually other architects."

In the case of Pilot Field, that concerned minority is baseball fans, tired of the awful sameness of so much ballpark design. The criticism of enclosed spaces, such as Three Rivers Stadium and Riverfront Stadium and such older places as Anaheim Stadium, is aesthetic (they all look the same), functional (the enclosure of Anaheim affected players' visual and physical balance and impaired their timing, leverage, rhythm, and reaction time), and psychological (the sameness robs the visitor of a sense of where he is). However, Buffalo's experiment proves that modern stadium design can be respectful of the city itself and of the needs of the game.

The Great Satchel Pa...

INNING 7

MAKING THE TEAM

Well-to-do ladies, mothers, and working girls with rough and blackened fingertips were among the thousands who swelled New York's Polo Grounds in 1885. Even as they stood on their seats and "brandished fans in ecstasies of applause", a darker element lurked on the streetcorners of Gotham, a plague, it was reported, of "that class of female gamblers and sporting women that has grown so considerable in New York City of late years".

A class of female tramps was reported to be travelling the southern countryside of America, challenging local men's teams to exhibition matches and inviting them back to their hotel rooms. Their behaviour on board trains was so scandalous that they were invited to remove themselves on several occasions.

Even the better class of woman, the "gentle creature", found herself swept into the maelstrom of uncontrolled emotion. A lady of Atlanta coming from the ballgrounds on a Peachtree streetcar began to abuse the umpire:

"Oh, he is awful mean," she said. "He just cheated us out of the game. My but wouldn't I like to have him here."

"I think you don't know what you are talking about," responded a lady of equal social status from Augusta. "That umpire was just as fair as he could be."

"He wasn't," responded the red-faced Atlantan.

"He was, I say he was," replied the Augustinian, clenching her fist.

"And I say you don't know what you are saying," answered Atlanta, rising to her feet.

"I guess I do," answered Augusta, rising in turn.

Atlanta raised her parasol while Augusta's gloved hand grabbed her rival by the shoulder.

A gentleman, at this instance, stepped between the two and reminded them of their proper station. At this, they fell back into their seats and daubed their eyes with lace handkerchiefs.

The Sporting Life of Philadelphia, in the quaint style of the day, not only told of women's interest in baseball, but provided sometimes comical, usually ugly, accounts of how other disenfranchised groups indulged in the national pastime.

A barnstorming team of Chinese players, for instance, was the subject of

Opposite: "I ain't ever had a job. I just always played baseball"—Satchel Paige.

curious stares and ridicule. And when they all went on strike in 1883, sympathy was extended by the sporting papers to their enterprising manager for the behaviour of the Lungs, One to Nine, and their substitute, Wash Tub Tommy. The night after winning weekly raises of ten to twenty dollars, the Lungs and Tommy sat in secret session in Two Lungs' Laundry, and it was reported that their laughter could be heard out on the sidewalk.

It says much about the magic theatre of baseball that it drew teams of players from those social groups barred from full participation in the everyday life of North America. Were they compensating for their isolation by creating for themselves a pitiful and second-rate identification with nineteenth-century norms? Were they performing a kind of elaborate parody of the popular white man's game? Or did their interest and involvement signify a deeper feeling for the game's roots and universal character?

The third explanation seems the most plausible one, if only because the baseball frenzy of these groups persisted long after they had gained a measure of acceptance in mainstream culture.

The teams of female tramps gave way to the only slightly less provocative bloomer girls who toured in the early decades of the twentieth century. Bloomer girls derived their name from the "uniform of liberation" (a kind of Turkish pantaloon) devised by feminist Amelia Jenks Bloomer in the 1850s. Mixed barnstorming teams came into their own in the first decade of the twentieth century; the Texas Bloomer Girls had seven women, four men, and a one-armed male centre-fielder. And, according to the manager of the New England Bloomer Girls, "Clarence Wortham was as handsome a girl as any boy on the team." There were as many champion bloomer-girl teams as there were entrepreneurs with the moxie to send them on the road. The women who played were tough-minded realists who had left behind constraining decorum when they started on the road.

The New York Bloomer Girls ended a 1913 tour in Raleigh, North Carolina, by trashing a hotel, demolishing windows, mirrors, and chairs. They then turned on the hotel owner and the town's police officer, beating them back with bats and balls.

Bloomer Girls: A Manitoba Presbyterian church ladies' baseball team, June 15, 1921.

"The female has no place in baseball, except to the degradation of the game. For two seasons now, various sections of the country have been nauseated with the spectacle of these tramps who have been repeatedly stranded and the objects of public charity. The girls are from 15 to 19 years of age, jaunty in style, brazen in manner and peculiar in dress"—The Sporting Life *of Philadelphia, 1885. This photo is of another young ladies' baseball club from 1890.*

As early as 1890, the following advertisement appeared in *The New York World* proposing the idea of a women's league:

> Wanted—50 girls to play base ball; $5 to $15 per week and all expenses; long engagement to travel to experienced players; ladies' league of 4 to 6 clubs now organizing for 1891; must be young, not over 20, good looking and good figure. Call Monday or Tuesday, 2 to 6 p.m., to Mr. Franklin at Dramatic Agency, 1162 Broadway, or 8 to 10 p.m. at 158 West 50th Street. Applicants outside of city must send photo, which will be returned.

The World, in response, noted caustically, "There is a movement afoot to degrade baseball by organizing a number of baseball clubs with women players."

Actual playing experience rather than physiological inferiority was the factor most likely to separate boys from girls and, with at least a grudging accord given to women's baseball in this era, it was hardly surprising that some of their number would challenge the male exclusivity of organized baseball. In 1898, Lizzy Arlington joined the minor-league team in Reading, Pennsylvania, and wore a grey uniform with skirt to the knees. It was reported that her hair was styled in the latest fashion. She played like a professional, even spitting on her hands and wiping them on her uniform.

In 1936, Frances (Sonny) Dunlop, an All-American basketball player, joined the Fayetteville Bears for their Class-D Arkansas–Missouri League season final game with the Cassville Blues. Dunlop went zero for three though it was reported that a Cassville centre-fielder made a fine running catch of Miss Dunlop's long fly ball.

In 1952, the Harrisburg Senators of the Inter State League attempted to sign Eleanor Engle, a twenty-four-year-old stenographer at the State Capitol; however, George Trautman, head of baseball's minor-league association, barred the signing of women players, and major-league commissioner Ford Frick voiced his assent. *The Sporting News* reported that "President Bill Veeck of the St. Louis Browns, who had presented a midget in a game and tried many bizarre promotional stunts, declared it was going too far." Unlike the midget, however, Mrs. Engle was a competent player and announced her intention to try out for the Fort Wayne Daisies of the All American Girls Professional Baseball League.

Within organized baseball, as male-oriented as any tribal patriarchy, one of the first women of major influence was Helene Britton, niece of St.

Louis Cardinals' owner Stanley Robison, who inherited the team in 1911 on his death. Sportswriter Fred Lieb described her as "a striking looking woman, a real beauty, with plenty of style, snap and sparkle. She was a militant rooter for women in suffrage and she plunged actively into the affairs of the St. Louis ballclub.... Mrs. B. was the real head and made all important decisions.... Sometimes accompanied by male associates, sometimes alone, she represented her club at all National League meetings in New York for the next six years. Dressed in the height of fashion, she didn't miss a league session in the years the club was hers."

As players, however, women's role in baseball awaited the somewhat golden years of the 1940s and 1950s. At this time, women's baseball was largely dominated by the bloomer girls' barnstorming successors, softball squads with oddly suggestive names—Dr. Pepper Girls of Miami Beach and Slapsie Maxie's Curvaceous Cuties.

In 1942, Phil Wrigley, the chewing-gum mogul and owner of the Chicago Cubs, alarmed at the declining quality of play in the National League as young ballplayers went off to war, got together with Branch Rickey of the Brooklyn Dodgers to discuss their options.

Ann Harnett, a tall redhead and organizer of women's softball for the Chicago playground system, became their adviser, consultant, and eventually a player. They first considered a superior softball league to improve the somewhat tarnished image of that girls' game. Wrigley, however, doubted that large numbers of spectators would accept what were traditionally low-scoring games with lots of strikeouts.

The underhand game was accordingly revised. Bases were placed seventy feet apart, a compromise between baseball (ninety feet) and softball (fifty-five feet); the pitching distance of forty-three feet was less than baseball's sixty feet but more than softball's thirty-five feet; and a special eleven-inch ball, smaller than a softball but bigger than a baseball, was used. Another change allowed pitchers a sidearm motion. As was the case in men's baseball in the nineteenth century, the form of the game was clearly a transitional one.

Wrigley's most bizarre innovation and, in retrospect, the one the players still question, was his emphasis on femininity. He wanted pretty, long-haired, All-American girls. Brash, overly masculine women were forbidden, as was the chewing of Wrigley's gum. Helena Rubenstein's products and the Ruth Tiffany Charm School were recruited to promote health, glamour, physical perfection, vim, vigour, and a sparkling personality.

That Wrigley also demanded a high standard of play led to some strange contradictions.

"I could see that some of us could use a little polish, but it was hard to walk on high heels with a book on your head when you had a charley horse," said Pepper Davis, a shortstop and catcher, in a half-hour video called *A League of Their Own*, which was shown on the American Public Broadcasting System in 1987.

And Dottie Schroeder, the only woman to play the full twelve seasons of the league from 1943 to 1954, said, "You went out there on the ball diamond like any other human being and got hot and dirty like everyone else. Charm School was mainly treated as a joke, it was a promotional deal."

Players who forgot their makeup were reprimanded. "It was sickening," Irene Hickson, the league's oldest player, said. "How could you wear all that makeup and your hair all the way up the way they wanted you to and get out there and play ball? Some of us didn't look any better if we had makeup on. But everyone felt there was something wrong with

The Eager Beavers: A Canadian Women's Armed Forces team playing in Holland at the end of the Second World War.

you because you could play ball. You were masculine and all that stuff...."

Wrigley's recruiters found many good players in Canada. The Sunday Morning Class team in Toronto once played an exhibition game against DiMaggio's Yankees in 1941. Thelma Golden, who once pitched five no-hit, no-run games in succession, and Gladys "Terry" Davis (no relation to Pepper), a good batter, were both signed. While Golden's deliveries were not effective and she soon went home, Davis became a fiery competitor who developed well-publicized rivalries.

She won the inaugural batting title with a .332 average, based on 349 at-bats in 102 games. With her husband overseas in the air force and her brother a prisoner of war in Germany, baseball provided a lucrative distraction, if only for one season.

League membership was the highlight of many lives; it provided women a chance to live somewhat independently, make fifty to eighty dollars a week, and play the game they loved. Helen Callaghan was allowed to go as long as her sister Marge accompanied her. So the two former stars of Vancouver's city league became the league's first family act. Helen's husband accepted his wife's rather unusual line of work: "He knew I was a ballplayer. And so we had a lady take care of my son and after the ballgame we were a family."

Baseball allowed a lifestyle that many women found liberating. Pepper Davis recalled: "I had a boyfriend in every port. Only one time did I ever get caught. This was in the days of gas rationing so you didn't expect to see someone you knew in one town show up in another. But in this game in Grand Rapids one of my teammates and I looked up and there sat four guys we knew. Well that type of thing wasn't done in our day, but we handled it like big leaguers. We hid under the grandstand."

Davis was not alone. Faye Dancer said, "I more or less did what I wanted and believe me that was a lot. I was always breaking the rules.

"There was this little midget fellow in Fort Wayne who brought us beer. We lived by the river, and he'd bring a case every night unless he saw the chaperone's green Ford coupe sitting in the dark outside the house. We'd go out to the graveyard and drink beer and talk late into the night. We were young then. We'd speak to the tombstones, waiting for them to speak back, I guess. We couldn't drink in public."

Other women used the experience as an opportunity to develop careers. Though the league's franchises were limited to the American midwest, Mary "Bonnie" Baker from Regina achieved national prominence. Her appearance on "What's My Line" nearly stumped the panel. In the off-season she was a highly successful model. Perhaps her outstanding achievement was a brief appointment as manager of the Kalamazoo Lassies in 1950. Until then, managerial ranks were the private preserve of former major-league players, among them Dave Bancroft, Marty McManus, Max Carey, and Jimmie Foxx.

"I played most of my career with the South Bend Blue Sox but they sent me over to Kalamazoo in mid season when their manager was fired," Baker recalled. "They asked me to finish the season and afterwards offered me another contract. But at a meeting in Chicago the league vetoed it. I understood their decision. They didn't want me managing and possibly beating former big league stars."

Baker was later employed as Canada's first woman radio sportscaster in the 1950s and then managed a curling rink in Regina. More than three decades after her playing career ended, both the Saskatchewan Sports Hall of Fame and the Saskatchewan Baseball Hall of Fame honoured her as an inductee.

Olive Bend Little of Poplar Point, Manitoba, was another league star.

Pam Postema.

Selected for the first all-star team in 1943, she also pitched the league's first no-hitter. The Rockford, Illinois, Peaches twice honoured her with Olive Little nights. "The Chicago writers all said I was quite a pitcher," Little said. "The rules gradually switched to hardball but I always kept to the underarm pitch. I guess I was lucky; I had a father and two brothers who kept after me. It's a good thing I could pitch because I couldn't hit the ball much further than the infield."

The players found that the league game offered a better balance of offence and defence than softball had, and they participated in its gradual evolution towards true baseball. By 1948, the league had adopted overhand pitching; over the next few years the distance between bases stretched to 85 feet (5 feet less than regulation), and 60 feet (6 inches less than regulation) from home plate to the pitcher's plate. Mary Baker owns four different-sized balls that were used over time in the league. As the ball shrunk in size, there were more home runs, more double plays, more hitting in general, and fewer stolen bases.

In 1946, in proportion to its population base and schedule length, the league outdrew major-league baseball. In South Bend, 113,000 jammed the turnstiles, including a record 7,800 for a game against Racine. Grand Rapids surpassed South Bend, and Muskegon (population 80,000) drew 140,000 for season and playoff games.

The 120-game schedule began in late March or April and continued through to the Labour Day playoffs. One notable magazine account told of a Saskatchewan ballplayer mushing three days by dogsled to make a rail connection that would take her to the league's spring-training site in Mississippi. "One year we went to Cuba for spring training," Faye Dancer recalled, "and they had to hire tourist cops to look after us. It was wild. The men loved blonde-haired people. My brother was fighting in the South Pacific but I think my mother got more grey hairs over what I did."

Their uniform consisted of a neat one-piece tunic cut off above the knees. Many of the players who refused to wear sliding pads tore up their thighs breaking up double plays at second base. As for equipment, Helen Callaghan remembered using a 36-ounce bat she got from a coach at Notre Dame. The game looked and was played just like its male major-league counterpart. According to league president Max Carey, "Actually girls are slower than men. But by putting our bases 72 feet apart, fixing our pitching distance at 50 feet and using a ball that's not quite as lively as that big league jackrabbit, our girls play baseball that looks as fast as a major league game on a 90 foot diamond." Carey's description applied to the league's inaugural season. In later years, the move towards men's rules became more pronounced.

After the immediate postwar boom and with the emergence of television and new lifestyles in the 1950s, interest in minor-league baseball declined, cutting into the All American Girls' attendance levels. Mary Baker, Helen Callaghan, and Olive Little were three of many who went home to raise families.

The league folded at the end of the 1954 season. Joanne Winter, who shared the single-season pitching victory record (thirty-three), became a professional golfer. Dottie Schroeder barnstormed across America with the Allington All Americans, a group of former league stars. In 1954, she played for the Kalamazoo All City men's squad against the Grand Rapids Black Sox.

None of these women ever played a major-league game, though Charlie Grimm, manager of the Chicago Cubs, declared after watching Kenosha shortstop Dottie Schroeder, "I'd pay $50,000 for her if she were a boy."

The All American Girls league continues to influence women's images

THE CHICAGO AND ALL-AMERICA TEAMS READY FOR PLAY AT VILLA BORGHESE, ROME.

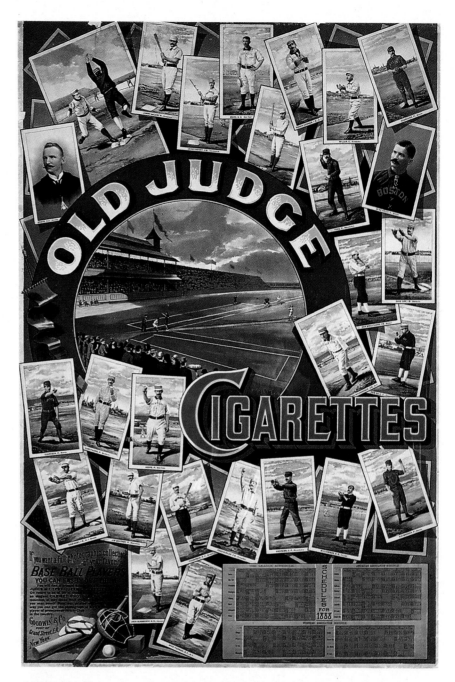

Old Judge Cigarettes advertising poster from the late nineteenth century.

Preceding:

The term "World Series", in use since the 1880s, is associated with the annual fall classic, begun in 1903. Ring Lardner comically dubbed it the "world serious".

From the Sphinx to the Villa Borghese, the whole world has been a stage for barnstorming American players.

Baseball stars of the 1950s and 1960s in miniature collectible form. Left to right: Nellie Fox, Warren Spahn, Willie Mays, Ed Matthews, Yogi Berra, Stan Musial.

Mechanical banks, metal games, and Lawson cards were some of the earliest baseball collectibles.

of themselves and of baseball. Players began to attend reunions in the 1980s and, inspired by memories of their exploits, Darlene Mehrer of Chicago founded the two-team American Women's Baseball Association in 1988. While not quite up to major-league rules (games last seven innings; stealing is banned; the pitching distance is fifty feet; and bases are eighty feet apart), the game is hardball.

Even in enlightened times, no one has illusions about the likelihood, practicality, or wisdom of women playing major-league baseball in the near future. However, some of the barriers may at last be falling.

In 1977, Pam Postema graduated from Al Sauer's umpire school. By 1983, she had climbed to the Triple-A level in the Pacific Coast League and, by 1988, was behind the plate for major-league preseason games. Her hair was kept short to fit under the umpire's cap, and her working voice was gutteral. "I umpire because I love the game," she said, "and because it's a challenge." Praised for observing a consistent strike zone, she withstood the taunts of such ballpark "wits" as the fan who called, "Get the woman back there. She's got a nicer butt"—not the stuff she might wish to hear on the street but, within the confines of baseball, a begrudging endorsement.

When Montreal fans mobbed Jackie Robinson following their city's Little World Series triumph in 1946, a Louisville sportswriter declared it was probably the only day in history that a black man ran from a white mob that had love rather than lynching on its mind.

Separate women's leagues could at least be rationalized on the basis of skill. For another group of ballplayers, no such excuse was acceptable. The history of baseball's treatment of blacks is clouded and tragic. When Los Angeles Dodgers executive Al Campanis rejected blacks as capable administrators in a televised interview before the 1987 season (for, among other "reasons", their inability to swim), he was espousing what many have assumed to be baseball's party line.

Among the first blacks in organized baseball of any form was Simpson Younger, son of a white slave owner and a black slave. Younger played for Oberlin College from 1867 to 1870 against such professional clubs as Forest City of Cleveland, and later became a gifted poet and scholar and sued the State of Missouri over its racist laws.

Sol White, a graduate of Wilberforce University, played in the white minor leagues as late as 1895 and in the Colored National League of 1887. He later managed several black teams and wrote a history of Negro baseball.

Younger and White, with college backgrounds, were exceptions among black players, but in the most profound sense, there were no exceptions insofar as black players were considered to be second-class citizens in their own country.

Participation by black athletes in baseball probably goes back to the 1850s, but records are scarce. The national amateur association in the United States banned blacks just two years after the Civil War ended. Despite resistance, however, the professional ranks were perhaps slightly more enlightened.

Bud Fowler, born John Jackson in the middle of the century, played independent and organized ball across the United States and Canada. His stops included Guelph, Ontario, in the early 1880s, where the members of the local team refused to play with him, forcing him to seek employment in Petrolia, Ontario. In early March 1884, he got to Stillwater, Minnesota, roomed at the Live and Let Live House, and did some barbering on the side, hoping, one assumes, to make himself known before any trouble could start. In 1887, he reached the highest category of minor-league ball, playing for Binghamton in the International League. In thirty-four games, he hit .350 and, in late May, won a life-sized portrait, the prize given to the player with the highest batting average during a week-long period.

In July of that year, however, International League officials, meeting in Buffalo, resolved to settle the question of black players. Noting that an alarming number of white players were threatening to quit the league, they decided "to approve no more contracts with colored men".

It is likely that this minor-league decision was precipitated by an action of Cap Anson's: on July 14, 1887, he cajoled the Newark team of the International League to drop Moses Walker and George Stovey from their lineup before Chicago would play their exhibition match. There was nothing in the relationship between majors and minors that guaranteed that intimidation would be successful. If anything, this was a case where strong moral leadership by the minors might have influenced, in time, the more narrow-minded point of view of the big leagues. Just such a stand had been taken in 1883 by Toledo of the Northwestern League, whose lineup included the same Moses Walker, when they responded to a similiar threat by Anson that his team would not play by stating that no guarantee would be paid if they did not do so. Anson changed his tune and Walker played right field for Toledo. The next season, when Toledo joined the American Association, Moses and his brother Welday were members of their team.

The post–Civil War period was a decisive one in American history. The tentative gains made by blacks as a result of the war were being eroded by the gradual spread of Jim Crow legislation that effectively banned them from participation in the mainstream of American life. The International League really sealed the fate of black players. With two Canadian members, in Toronto and Hamilton, and members in such northern industrial cities as Buffalo, Rochester, and Syracuse, one might have expected this league to be free of the more southerly intolerance. Such was not the case, however, and some players, second baseman Frank Grant of Buffalo, George Stovey of Newark, and Fleet Walker of Newark and Syracuse, for example, were eventually banned. Walker was the last black in the league, playing fifty games in the 1889 season. To help confuse the issue, he and George Stovey had identified themselves as Cubans and Buffalo's Frank Grant was described as an Italian. The constant threat of attack forced Walker to carry a gun, which he once turned on a Hamilton, Ontario, publisher who had printed a freelance writer's ugly story about "coon baseball".

Walker was often quoted in the sporting papers, decrying the black man's restricted situation, but the forces against black participation were growing. When John Montgomery Ward wanted to sign George Stovey with the Giants, the weight of the game was brought against him.

Blacks were forced to resort to the rigours of barnstorming tours under such names as the Cuban Giants (a team first formed by the workers at a Long Island hotel), and these black teams sent letters to all-white teams in search of exhibition encounters. The St. Louis Black Sox manager wrote in one such request: "We have organized the only club of professional colored ballplayers in the country and intend making an extended tour, knowing that a colored team will be a novelty as well as a new enterprise."

Many white stars of the age, such as Cap Anson of Chicago and Tip O'Neill of St. Louis, refused to play in exhibition matches against all-black teams. To counter such opposition, the League of Colored Baseball Clubs was formed in 1887, with teams in New York, Philadelphia, Boston, and other big cities. The previous year had seen the formation of a Southern League of Colored Base Ballists, with teams in Memphis, Atlanta, Savannah, Charleston, Jacksonville, and New Orleans. Neither league survived for long.

Martin Dihigo, great Cuban star and 1977 Hall of Fame inductee.

The Page Fence Giants, an early black barnstorming team.

By the early twentieth century, black participation in organized baseball was over and a new era of play had begun. Some itinerant black teams traversed the nation, often to places where blacks had not been before. For the players, it was a spirited if troubling existence.

The black community itself had mixed feelings about this "show". In a bid to increase the gates, some teams experimented with comedy stunts during the game. By the 1920s, Nat Strong, who booked black teams' games in New York, forbade those comedy teams from playing in the city. "You don't see major leaguers clowning," he said.

In some ways, the joke was on the audience. Chappie Johnson, whose touring team became the fictional staple of Canadian novelist John Craig's *Chappie and Me*, recognized the peculiar dynamic of these games. "He always tried to win by a few runs," Craig noted. "Any more and the crowd got restless, too few and Chappie got nervous probably because he had a bet on the outcome." Humour was a means of keeping the home fans' minds off the final result.

In the larger American cities, black teams that played straight rather than as comedy were sponsored by such booking agents as Nat Strong, a liberal white who was described in a black newspaper as "a very broad minded man of wide experience. He holds the friendship of some of the greatest stars that the race has produced."

Support came not only from blacks but from such prominent socialists as American artist John Sloan. Sloan, at the time a contributor to leading leftist journals, regularly attended games played by the Black Giants of New York, as recorded in his diaries from 1906 to 1913. His guest on at least one occasion was John Butler Yeats, father of the Irish poet W.B. Yeats.

Sloan recalled a game on July 17, 1910, when Walter Schlicter called and asked Yeats and Sloan up to 135th Street and Lennox Avenue to see a game between his Giants of Philadelphia and the Royal Giants: "both [were] 'colored' teams and the field is right in the heart of the colored district up in Harlem, the people mostly black and well dressed and of splendid behaviour. Mr. Yeats was immensely delighted with the afternoon, he had never seen a game of baseball before. The Phila. Giants won in a hotly contested battle. We thanked Schlicter for a pleasant afternoon and went down to Petitpas' for dinner with Mr. Yeats!"

This game was one of the many that Sloan attended, often stopping on the way to leave copies of the socialist weekly on the benches near Madison Square Garden, "in the fond hope of spoiling someone's peace of mind". Often he and his wife, Dolly, would join Nat Strong for dinner."

In 1920, former player "Rube" Foster organized the Negro National League, which finally brought some stability to black baseball. He had once pitched with the Cuban and Philadelphia Giants and managed the Chicago Leland Giants to a 123–6 record in 1910. A year later, he took over the presidency of the Chicago American Giants.

Foster got his nickname when he was a pitcher with the independent team that beat the famed Rube Waddell and the Philadelphia Athletics in New York. He was an ambitious and imaginative promoter who, until his illness in 1926, dominated league proceedings. When one owner, John Matthews of the Dayton Marcos, dozed off in a meeting, he awoke to find his franchise dissolved and his players distributed among rival teams.

According to historian Donn Rogosin, a baseball team's role in building community spirit was unrivalled: "In cities where blacks were largely first generation immigrants from the South, the teams evolved into a vital component of community building and a city without a Negro League team was almost by definition a second rate black community."

In Pittsburgh, such clubs as the 18th Ward, the Garfield Eagles, and the Crawfords tied together neighbourhoods and gradually came to represent the larger black community between the wars.

In Kansas City, the Monarchs were arguably the greatest black team of all time, once winning forty-two straight in 1932. On the other hand, they were also victims of "Smokey" Joe Williams's twenty-seven strikeouts in a ten-inning game in 1930. Their most famous graduate, of course, was to be Jackie Robinson.

Even in the best of times, the Negro Leagues depended on sometimes unexpected, sometimes notorious sources of backing. Gus Greenlee created the Pittsburgh Crawfords from the profits of his numbers racket. He had made his reputation in the 1920s after being the only numbers banker to pay off after a large hit. As a successful businessman, he was just naturally expected to support the community.

Effa Manley in Newark was perhaps the league's most respected owner. Player Jimmy Wilkes said: "She was a beautiful lady. When I got started, Bill Cash [a catcher with the Negro League Philadelphia Stars from 1943 to 1950] told the Philadelphia Stars that I could play the outfield for them but their manager said I was too small. Bill called Newark and Mrs. Manley told me to come up. She gave me a tryout and I was her centerfielder after that. Monte Irvin [a future New York Giant] was on one side of me but she told him that if Jimmy says he's got it, then you let him take it."

It is doubtful, however, that the game would have survived without the personalities of some truly gifted performers. The greatest stars were always being held up to the light of their white major-league counterparts. Josh Gibson, for instance, was the "Babe Ruth of Negro baseball"; Buck Leonard was its Lou Gehrig; John Henry Lloyd, its Honus Wagner. In the absence of solid statistics, their game developed an almost mythic quality.

James "Cool Papa" Bell, inducted into the Hall of Fame in 1974.

The Pittsburgh Crawfords, champions of the Negro National League, 1935.

Tales that could not be true mingled with those close to everyday fact to elevate the game to the stuff of folk legend.

One wants to believe, for instance, the story told by Tom Baird, an owner of the Kansas City Monarchs, that he once saw southpaw John Donaldson strike out twenty-seven batters, or Buck O'Neil's memory of Oscar Charleston, that "he was so strong he could take a ball in his hand, twist it and turn the cover." Some accounts are wonderfully unbelievable.

"How fast was Cool Papa Bell?" Satchel Paige was asked. "One time he hit a line drive past my ear. I turned around and the ball hit his ass sliding into second."

How strong was Josh Gibson? According to Paige, Gibson hit a home run in Pittsburgh's Forbes Field that went so high, no one saw it come down and the umpire called it a home run. The next day in Philadelphia, a ball dropped from the sky into a fielder's glove. The ump pointed at Gibson and shouted, "Yer out—yesterday in Pittsburgh."

How fast was Paige? Biz Mackey, an outstanding catcher, replied, "I've heard about Satchel throwing pitches that wasn't hit but that never showed up in the catcher's mitt. They say the catcher, the umpire, and the bat boys looked all over for that ball but it was gone."

At the centre of these great fables was Satchel Paige, a pitcher who guessed that, in a career that began professionally in 1926 and lasted until 1965 when, at age fifty-nine, he pitched a couple of innings for the Kansas City As, he had been on the mound in 2,500 games. In the 1930s, he pitched for the Pittsburgh Crawfords in the Negro Leagues and barnstormed in the off-season, billing himself as the World's Greatest Pitcher, guaranteed to strike out the first nine men he faced. When he finally joined the major-league Cleveland Indians in 1948, he was a forty-two-year-old veteran.

Paige was as famous for his philosophy—"Don't look back, something might be gaining on you"—as for his unorthodox pitching style. According to Jimmy Wilkes, who played in the Negro Leagues in the 1940s, "We always knew when Satch was going to pitch because he'd take infield practice over by third base. He never warmed up. He had pinpoint control and sometimes he'd tease a batter by throwing three balls and then put the ball where he wanted for three strikes."

His hesitation pitch, in which he paused in his motion as his left foot hit the ground, so baffled batters' timing that the American League banned it.

By the late 1930s, the movement towards integrating the major leagues was gaining momentum. The black community put pressure on the Pirates to give Josh Gibson and Buck Leonard a tryout, but nothing happened. Among baseball officials, there was tremendous reluctance to be the first.

Tragically, stars such as Josh Gibson would never get a shot at the big leagues. No one will ever know how many home runs Gibson actually hit but his strength in all facets of the game was extraordinary. "I remember playing the Homestead Grays one night in Griffith Stadium," Jimmy Wilkes recalled. "Gibson was near the end of his career and my manager said he couldn't throw anyone out. He gave me the go ahead to steal. I got on base and, on the first pitch, took off for second. The ball was waiting for me.

"Another time we played his team in Yankee Stadium. Gibson hit a ball on a line and I had to go around the monuments to get that ball."

In 1945, Branch Rickey, president of the Brooklyn Dodgers, moved quickly to get the jump on fellow owners in recruiting blacks. On May 7, he announced formation of the six-team United States Negro Baseball League as a cover for an even more audacious move—the signing of a black man to a Brooklyn contract. Rickey's motives have been seen by some as merely self-serving and, in a way, unethical, considering the token payments for players made to the owners of Negro League teams. In some cases, however, the ends were more important than the means. In 1945, Hector Racine of the Montreal Royals (members, ironically, of the International League, which had banned black players in 1887) announced that Jackie Robinson would play for his team the next season. The Royals were the chief farm team of the Dodgers; if Robinson made good here, the integration of the majors was next on the agenda.

Some writers said Montreal had been selected because Canada was free of racial intolerance. In Montreal itself, there were few blacks to be discriminated against and the Robinsons were something of a novelty. "The first apartment that I said I wanted," Rachel Robinson recalled, "I got. That alone was very exciting."

Robinson met all expectations. Not only did he put up with the occasional racist taunts by fans and other players but he led the Royals to the championship of minor-league baseball. By season end, he was a hero in Montreal. A Louisville sportswriter suggested it was the first time a black man had been chased down the street out of love rather than hate. The next year, fully seven years before the Supreme Court's Brown v. Board of Education decision ushered in the civil-rights era, Jackie Robinson was the starting first baseman for the Brooklyn Dodgers. He hit .297, stole a league-leading 29 bases, and won grudging admiration from formerly uncertain teammates for his restraint in the face of threats from rival teams.

The Boston Red Sox were the last team to integrate their lineup, in the late 1950s, and Frank Robinson became baseball's first black manager in 1975. The Negro Leagues petered out by the 1960s, and the last great black barnstorming team, the Indianapolis Clowns, continued for twenty years on the road with black and white players.

With the entry of many of the great black ballplayers, including Paige, Gibson, Bell, Foster, Leonard, and Dandridge, into baseball's Hall of Fame, the inglorious past was, if not expunged, then at least acknowledged in a most poignant way.

Jackie Robinson's entry into the major leagues was one case in which the game did not simply reflect the social reality of the times but, in fact, led it into a new era. Bob Kent, a Canadian baseball fan, recalls visiting

The Kansas City Monarchs preparing for the Negro World Series in the 1920s.

Pittsburgh in 1947. He and his friends stood to cheer Robinson when he hit a home run only to notice that the rest of the white fans were not only seated but casting unfriendly glances in their direction. Thirty-five years later, the exploits of Roberto Clemente and Willie Stargell had become so much a part of that city's heritage that one could only wonder why baseball had waited so long.

While the game has been noticeably slower in advancing blacks through its management ranks, nothing can take away from that great moment when Jackie Robinson first stepped onto a major-league field and put to rest at last the troubled soul of Moses Walker.

INNING 8

AROUND THE WORLD

Albert Spalding was convinced that the 1888–89 South Pacific tour of two teams of major-league ballplayers would convince Australians that baseball was the game of the future. Assured of the sport's merits, he would, in mid-voyage, take the final leap of faith in this belief and decide to take the entire party of travellers round the world. Spalding was a classic nineteenth-century entrepreneurial positivist. To him, commerce and idealism were faithful partners, and it was as much for the love of the game as out of a desire to market baseball products outside North America that he devoted his considerable talents to making baseball international. The acceptance of baseball as an official sport of the 1992 Olympic Games marks the ultimate realization of Spalding's dream.

The heritage of baseball, as noted earlier, is broadly international, but there were two means by which the game was given back, as it were, to the rest of the world in the last century. One route was indirect, through the auspices of the military, schoolteachers, and missionaries from America on foreign assignments, and was aided by visitors to the United States who brought word of the game back to their native lands. The other was deliberate; such operations as the 1874 tour of England, the first such baseball trip by American players, and Spalding's round-the-world adventure were marked by the curious ability of the imperialist to recreate any landscape in an image of home and to use foreign property as mere backdrop for his play—in this case, baseball.

In the nearly thirty years since baseball as an adult sport was formalized and taken seriously by the general public, the game had grown from a gentleman's pastime to a proud if still somewhat befuddled business. It was said that Al Spalding (born in Byron, Illinois, and in 1874, a twenty-three-year-old pitcher for the Boston Red Stockings of the National Association of Professional Base Ball Players) had always wanted to see England. Spalding had been much impressed by the tours of English cricketers to North America, including the brief tour in the winter of 1872 that had brought W.G. Grace, the great man of the English game, to Canada. That brief tour inspired Spalding; allied with two of America's prominent baseball exponents, fellow player Harry Wright and journalist Henry Chadwick (both born in England), he arranged for his own Boston team and the Philadelphia Athletics to make baseball's first grand excursion abroad. The Marylebone Cricket Club agreed to act as hosts when they learned that George and Harry Wright of the Boston team were sons of Sam Wright, a famous Nottinghamshire cricketer, who had gone to America forty years earlier.

Opposite: Baseball cheerleader performs dance of encouragement at Tokyo's Korakuen Stadium, 1975.

As it turned out, the English had little interest in the baseball exhibitions of their visitors and were somewhat lukewarm in attending cricket matches between the Americans and the English. Playing with eighteen men to the English eleven, the Americans were undefeated in their seven cricket matches (with three draws, including one against Marylebone), though their batting style horrified cricket purists. The cricketer defends the wicket by innocently deflecting away any on-target tosses and making a full, unrestrained swing only at off-target balls. Unaccustomed to such defensive posturing, the Americans took a cut at just about anything.

Of the fourteen baseball games played, *The Field* magazine derisively noted, "it has not the slightest pretension to be considered superior to...our own amusement, 'rounders', on the basis of which it has been modelled." And Stonehenge's *British Rural Sports Illustrated*, a 966-page compendium of sporting detail, said of baseball: "Last year an attempt was made to introduce it into this country, but its signal failure prevents any necessity for describing it here." Rebuffed but not defeated, Spalding had a larger purpose. He was to be instrumental in establishing the National League, organizing a world tour, and putting down the players' revolt of 1890. In 1906, he established a committee to prove that baseball had no connection to English rounders and succeeded in promoting this ruse. As recently as May 1987, a Cuban international magazine accepted the Spalding hoax.

The most fondly remembered of Spalding's trips was the grand adventure of 1888–89. By that time, baseball was a confident and successful enterprise, firmly established across all parts of the United States and in various stages of growth in parts of the Caribbean and as far away as Japan. Spalding himself was an established capitalist at the peak of his merchandising and baseball careers.

Spalding's World Tour may have been a public-relations bonanza back home, but its reception in the countries it visited was less enthusiastic. When a similar tour swept through Australia just before the First World War, it received polite and generally favourable attention from crowds of 10,000 spectators in Sydney and Melbourne, but there was little evidence that the Spalding tour had left much of an impression: the Americans outscored the Australians 42–1 in three games. When the expedition paid visits to Ceylon and Egypt, it found the same indifference Spalding had encountered twenty-five years earlier. The lack of interest spread to umpire Jack Sheridan, who missed passage out of Egypt with the others and did not catch up with them again until Italy. Rain wiped out engagements in Rome and Paris. The French press criticized the Americans' apparent unwillingness to play. If anything, the cause of European baseball had been set back beyond the gains Spalding had made.

Baseball's success outside the North American continent owed more to the seemingly innocent enthusiasm for the game instilled by visiting amateurs. Just after the Civil War, sailors on an American ship taking on sugar in the Cuban port of Matanzas Bay introduced the game to locals and then helped build a ballpark at Palmar del Junco. In the winter of 1874, Matanzas lost a game to Havana 51–9. Playing in that game was Esteban Bellan, a black player who had learned the game from Cuban students returning from American colleges and who subsequently spent three seasons (1871–73) in the National Association with the Troy Haymakers and the New York Mutuals. Another Havana player, Emilio Sabourin, organized the island's first pro league in 1878 and promoted not only baseball but Cuban independence from Spain. Money from baseball was funnelled to Cuban patriots such as poet José Martí, and the Spanish

Ballplayers in Paris, France, 1924.

eventually tried to ban the game. As early as 1879, they had objected to a baseball exhibition staged by a former Civil War veteran and future Detroit manager, Frank Bancroft. His touring team played anyway, despite accusations of cruelty—the sight of ballplayers sliding into base unnerved the Spanish.

In the Far East, a series of treaties negotiated between Japanese authorities and Western representatives opened six coastal ports for preferential trade. Americans and Europeans were granted almost absolute power to administer their own legal and political matters, and there soon evolved a rather independent enclave of foreign residents. Japan, in a period of transition from her feudal samurai past to a modern state, was training her youth in abstract intellectual pursuits rather than physical ones. Consequently, little interest was taken in 1864 when teams of the British army and navy played the first cricket match in Yokohama. Soon after, a Yokohama Athletic Club was formed and its one playing field was dominated by cricketers until the 1880s, when new American arrivals introduced baseball. In the early 1870s, three American teachers, Horace Wilson, G.H. Mudgett, and Leroy Janes, and an Englishman, F.W. Strange, had each tried to teach Japanese students the game, but it remained a novelty for much of the decade. In 1878, Hiraoka Hiroshi, a supervisor from the Ministry of Engineering who had studied in the United States, organized railway employees into what was probably the first Japanese baseball team.

By the 1880s, criticism of the lack of physical training for youths aged seventeen to twenty in higher schools had grown and outdoor games, including baseball, were introduced.

Baseball met a peculiar national need in Japan. Such sports as judo and kendo celebrated solitary virtues, but there was a need for collectivist recreation to mirror the traditional Japanese civic rituals of state that were based on order, harmony, perseverance, and self-restraint. Baseball was a perfect solution. While it was clearly a team game, enough emphasis was placed on the individual to satisfy the Japanese tradition. Batters were compared to samurai swordsmen, and baseball was said to represent "the new bushido" spirit of the age (the bushido was the code of honour of the samurai). Keio students organized a team in 1885 but lacked administrative support until 1893. The team of the First Higher School (Ichikō) of Tokyo (one of the five elite prep schools for the national university) was dominant in the fall of 1890 and one year later formally challenged the Yokohama Athletic Club to an international match (*kokusai shiai*). The Americans refused such challenges time and again, citing as an excuse, "baseball is our national game and our bodies are twice the size of yours." Finally, W.B. Mason, an English teacher at Ichikō, managed to arrange a game with the Yokohama club at their home field on May 23, 1896.

Negotiations to end the privileged status of Westerners were underway at the time, but one would not have known it from the jeering spectators who laughed at the smaller Japanese players. Right triumphed over might, however; Ichiko embarrassed the Americans 29–4.

Atsunori Ito of Japan's Olympic team.

Banzai chants, the national anthem, and glasses of sake awaited the players on their return, and the students proclaimed: "This great victory is more than a victory for our school; it is a victory for the Japanese people." (The elation—and shock—were comparable to those registered in 1950 when the United States soccer team defeated England 1–0 in the World Cup and in 1972 when the Russian hockey team defeated Canadian professionals in Montreal in the first of a best-of-eight series.) In a rematch one month later, the American team, bolstered by additions from two American cruisers moored in Yokohama harbour, lost again, 32–9. The Asahı newspaper trumpeted with front-page headlines: "A Great Victory for Our Students". Crowds began to line the streets to welcome the players as baseball was becoming a key symbol of Japan's national awakening. More than 10,000 spectators jammed the Ichiko school grounds several weeks later for a game against the sailors of the American cruiser *Detroit*. At Yokohama, locals had been barred from attending, but here their joy was unrestrained as the Japanese students won again, 22–6. Finally, an American team made up of players from the flagship of the Pacific fleet, the battleship *Olympia*, which included one former pro ballplayer, defeated the students 14–12 in a July 4 match in Yokohama. Soon after, a letter arrived from Yale University inviting the Japanese team to an intercollegiate tournament in the United States. Lack of funds prevented their attendance.

Baseball in Japan was now no longer merely recreational. ("The three years spent as a member of the Ichikō Baseball Club are years of total sacrifice," one student recalled.) At Waseda, the Christian socialist Abe Isoo, one of the school's most prominent faculty members and called by some, as a measure of respect more than influence, the "father of Japanese baseball", encouraged the development of a team in the early 1900s.

In the decade following the Russo-Japanese War (1904–05), teams from Waseda and Keio visited the United States, while American university teams, including one from Stanford, travelled to Japan. In 1909, a Japanese university team even visited London, England, but was perplexed by the

British interpretation of the game and the exchange went no further. By 1915, Lindsay Russell, president of the Japan Society, called the Ichikō–Yokohama series and the matches that followed a landmark in inter-Pacific relations.

World tours and missionaries aside, the most successful exporters of baseball were the American military. While tossing a ball at the Sphinx or trying to rent the Colosseum for a baseball match seem somewhat tasteless symbols of the travelling Americans' native chauvinism, they pale in comparison to the darker deeds of the armed forces.

Following the submission of the Chinese in the late nineteenth century, the British, with their cricket pitches in the Temple of Heaven, and then the Americans, with their ball games in the Temple of Earth, gave stunning demonstrations of their cultural imperialism. *Outing* magazine described one particular scene:

> Here in one of the most sacred and inviolable places of all China—a place for ages dedicated to an annual pilgrimage of solemn worship by the Emperor— a thousand lusty Americans were using the very altars for "bleachers" while they "rooted" for the rival nines of Riley's Battery and the Sixth Cavalry squadron. The American Army League was in full swing for the Peking championship, and the hoarse volleys of "Rotten umpire!" "Soak it to her, Kelly!" "Wow-w, slide, you lobster!" re-echoed from gray parapets that had never before been profaned by a foreigner.
>
> These Yankee exiles fell to "playing ball" as naturally as to foraging, and while they were engaged in driving the festive three-bagger through the startled air of North China, jackies in white duck were circling the bases in blazing Cuba and Honolulu, or landing from revenue-cutter patrols to stake out a home-plate on frozen Alaskan beaches; and soldier and sailor teams were swinging their bats from one end of the Philippines to the other. As the British drum-beat has encircled the globe, so has the slogan of "Play ball!" followed by the Stars and Stripes, proclaiming the reign of the finest outdoor game ever devised.

The military also strengthened the game's profile in Italy, where despite several tours of American professionals, baseball had few adherents. It had a short life in Turin and Rome in 1919 and again in the late 1930s, when Italian physical-education instructors were sent to the United States to learn the game. Italians faulted baseball for its complexity, calling the "4,000 rules" an encumbrance.

In 1944, Americans staggered ashore at Anzio and Nettuno under heavy Nazi fire, and within days, having secured a beachfront, were playing ball. One of the witnesses was a stubby Italian nobleman, Prince Steno Borghese, who thought the game a childish amusement, but, perhaps recognizing the winds of change, surrendered some of his beachside acreage to make one of Italy's first baseball diamonds. Within a decade, he was head not only of the Italian Baseball Federation but also of its European counterpart.

Volunteers from the American military, embassy officers, and black-robed seminarians helped spread the game. Their numbers included a former G.I., Horace McGarity, who returned to Nettuno in 1950 to oversee the cemetery for the American war dead. The local team, with McGarity as coach, won three of four national titles. When the American Battle Monuments Commission accused McGarity of borrowing Pentagon water sprinklers for use on Borghese's ball diamond, he was sent home.

Elsewhere, Milan's Baseball 46 club was named for the year in which the game caught on in that city. Emilio LePetit joined the club two years later as a player; forty years later, he was the club president.

By 1956, *Sports Illustrated* magazine was telling its readers that with 2,000 active players and 100,000 fans, "all with one eye on the U.S., the Communists have an enemy which is growing dangerously." The reference was, of course, to the enthusiasm for baseball that now reigned in Europe.

On that continent, a Dutch baseball federation had been formed in 1910, the Paris Ranelagh Club in 1913, and the Fédération Belge in 1923. In all such cases it seems appropriate to credit not only the two great tours but the older heritage of bat-and-ball games in Western Europe. Indeed, there is some suggestion that Cartwright's New York game is a descendant of early baseball-type games introduced to that city during the seventeenth-century Dutch occupation.

In 1924, a third American visit—this time by John McGraw's Giants and Charles Comiskey's White Sox—was made by American big-leaguers to Paris. A crowd of 10,000 filled the Stade de Colombes and, shortly thereafter, the Fédération Française de Baseball was formed, with McGraw and Comiskey as honorary vice-presidents. It was during the 1924 tour that George Bernard Shaw, writing about a game in London, declared that "baseball has the advantage over cricket of being over sooner."

Beginning in 1929, a series of international tournaments was held, featuring teams from Holland, France, Spain, Belgium, and Great Britain. While the rounders-based game continued in Wales and Liverpool, American baseball gained a following between the wars. Hull won the National Cup in 1937, defeating the Romford Wasps at Craven Park before more than 15,000 fans, many of whom had gained admission over the trampled fencing. At the amateur level, some fifty clubs were operating at this time, but the brief golden age ended with the Second World War and a British revival did not occur until the 1980s.

The development of videotaping and satellite television has reinforced the postwar spread of American culture, making it a world-wide phenomenon. American football has pressed into Britain and the continent, despite its having no heritage there on which to build. Baseball, which does have at least a minor foothold, has seen its popularity mushroom.

The Dutch dominated European baseball from the mid-1950s to the 1970s (even the great Dutch soccer player Johan Cruyff played the game). Holland sent the first European-trained ball player to the major leagues. Win Remmerswaal, born in The Hague in 1954, was recommended to the Boston Red Sox by Cees Herkemy, a coach in the Dutch Amateur Baseball Federation. Remmerswaal played for two Dutch Little League Champions and one Babe Ruth Champion, and in 1973, was on the Dutch All-Star team that won the European Amateur title. In two major-league seasons (1979 and 1980), his pitching record was 3–1.

By 1985, there were 13,000 baseball players in 200 clubs in the Netherlands. Ten clubs played a 36-game schedule on weekends from April until early September in the best division (called the "Hoofdklasse"). Amsterdam, Haarlem, The Hague, Utrecht, and Rotterdam were among the member cities. The Tijgers of Amstel came third in the 1987 European Cup and began constructing a multimillion-dollar baseball complex. The annual Haarlem Baseballweek has attracted college teams from around the world.

In France and her overseas territories, such as Tahiti, Martinique, and Corsica, there were 170 clubs in 1987, some with not only a major team and a reserve squad but a junior organization and a women's softball division as well. Olivier Dubaut, president of the French federation, claimed that

The 1937 Championship Baseball Team of New South Wales, Australia.

"the problem in France is no longer how to keep an interest in the sport going, it is how to accommodate the incredible explosion of enthusiasm that has overtaken the game—how to make sure that everyone who wants to play baseball has the chance to do so."

A typical game in Le Vélodrome au Bois de Vincennes, a large wooded park and grandstand on the outskirts of Paris, cost 25 francs a ticket in 1983 and regularly attracted 3,000 fans who listened to Buddy Holly and Del Shannon records during batting practice. Fans drank Heineken from the bottle and ate fresh baguettes trowelled with pâté, and Spalding gloves and baseballs were sold after the game.

In Italy, by 1987, there were 800 clubs, including 2,700 teams and 40,000 players. At the top of the heap are the twelve teams in Division A, the national division. In the late 1960s, American soldiers often provided the ablest outside competition, but the level of play is now so improved that, twenty years later, an American junior team from the U.S. Air Force base in Germany finished last in an amateur baseball tournament, losing to the host Parma team 23–13. As a result, those Americans who now fill out European professional lineups are often themselves former major- or minor-league players from the United States. The Parma Angels, winners of eight European Cups in an eleven-year span in the 1970s and 1980s, added pitcher Mike Pagnozzi and catcher Randy Hunt, a former Montreal Expo (1986). Perhaps the most notable American import was twelve-year (1971–82) major-league veteran Lenny Randle, who became a celebrity in Nettuno doubling as a radio disc jockey.

While some contemporary American big-leaguers are European-born, including Bert Blyleven (Holland, 1951) and Charlie Lea (Orléans, France, 1956), their training was American. Giorgio Castelli from Parma, however, was Italian trained; offered a contract by Cincinnati in the early 1960s, he declined, preferring to play the next twenty-three years for his home team.

An Italian game is stoked by national passions. Spectators arrive with baskets of fruit, cheese, bread, and wine, carrying pennants of their local team. Fireworks, bonfires, and men in thirteenth-century costume, carrying medieval pageant flags, often appear at special games. Chants resound throughout the game, more in tune with a European soccer match than an American baseball game, and while the players dress and field like big-leaguers, their hitting is weak, perhaps testimony to the contrast between baseball's demanding eye-hand co-ordination and soccer's agility.

As well as in these European strongholds, baseball has found new life in formerly untapped territory. In Switzerland, for instance, baseball had to contend with a landscape more suited to downhill skiing. The Swiss had seen the game on visits to the United States, but few gave thought to playing it within their own borders until 1980, when two rival gangs from Lucerne and Zurich met on a snowy December day, kitted out with equipment imported from Italy. Over the decade, teams were formed in Lugano, Zurich, Lucerne, Basel, Solothurn, and Aarau. Christian Burkhalter of the Zurich Challengers claimed never to have played before joining. "They gave me a rule book translated in German this thick," he said, indicating a three-inch span. "Too many rules. It's better to play and learn as we go along." As was true in the early days of baseball in America, the scores indicated the skill level. In their first season, the Aarau Hawks were walloped by Burkhalter's Challengers 40–1.

Even stranger, however, was the spread of the game to eastern Europe. Attempts had been made by YMCA instructors to introduce baseball into Czechoslovakia in 1930 but unlike basketball and volleyball, which were also taught, it was a singular failure. American soldiers played baseball in the western part of Czechoslovakia at the war's end, but the eventual Soviet lifestyle that permeated the country left no room for the game. By the late 1970s, students began to play baseball in Prague, with no gloves and the bare necessities of one ball and bat per team. In 1976, a Czech baseball and softball association was established. Games are played on soccer fields now, though several clubs plan to build more appropriate venues. While sports authorities preferred sports with stronger eastern European connections, they grudgingly accepted baseball when it was recognized as an Olympic demonstration sport in 1984 and 1988 and finally as an official sport for 1992.

Of perhaps greater significance to the advance of Czechoslovakian baseball was the gradual acceptance of the game in the Soviet Union in the mid-1980s. Describing a visit by his national team to Russia in 1987, Jan Bagin noted, "We won three and lost one game. The first game was won by the home team 5–4, with ten players. Number ten was the Russian umpire behind home plate."

A heritage of bat-and-ball games resides in Russia in the form of an antique game called *lapta*, a rounder-type game with roots traceable at least as far back as the thirteenth century. Interest in *lapta* waned at the beginning of the twentieth century, and despite the attempts of American expatriates to introduce it in the 1930s, baseball was ignored until recently. As happened when they adopted ice hockey after the war, the Russians have been methodical in their training. Sometimes the results are other than expected. One of the country's best pitchers, Yura Trifonyenko, threw so hard on a daily basis that he developed the pitcher's bane—a sore arm. Hitting a speeding ball with a thin piece of wood is also a task without precedence for Soviet youth. And while coaching has been provided by

Shanty Clifford, a Negro League player in the 1940s, shown playing in the Dominican Republic.

Cubans, Nicaraguans, and, in 1988, two Calgary coaches, Al Price and Al Herback, the game's play often resembles a typical little-league affair where the batter reaches first on a dropped third strike, steals second and third, and scores on either a wild pitch or a fielding error. In 1987, a junior team was embarrassed by a Nicaraguan squad, 22–0. In the far eastern city of Khabarovsk, however, the nearby Japanese have lent assistance and real baseball uniforms and there are efforts across the country to revive *lapta* at the juvenile level to teach basic bat-and-ball skills, much as t-ball has been developed in North America. And while the game has elements that remind one of a Westerner trying to eat with chopsticks, the Russians have set themselves a goal of participating in the 1996 Olympics.

Nicaraguans and Cubans, who are often the recipients of Russian aid, must secretly laugh at the reversal of roles baseball allows them. The perseverance of baseball in both countries despite their unfriendly relations with the United States testifies to the game's triumph as much more than one country's national pastime.

Baseball serves to support a national mythology in Nicaragua, where it was introduced by invading U.S. Marines early in the twentieth century. The Dantos club was formed in honour of guerrilla leader and baseball fan German Pomares, killed months before the Sandinistas overthrew the Somoza government in 1979. All ten teams in the Nicaraguan league are supported by the government, though it is generally assumed that Dantos, sponsored by the army, gets more than the others. As a result, more baseball fans cheer when Dantos is losing. In the 1988 final, a team from the Atlantic coast, the Costenos, went to seven games against Dantos.

The last game was an emotional affair, with 20,000 fans packing Ricardo Lopez Stadium in Nicaragua (once known as Anastasio Somoza Stadium, it was renamed in honour of his assassin). The final is always played in April, at the end of the dry season, and the ballpark is possibly the only green area in the city. Fans of Costenos beat Caribbean drums and danced to the reggae and calypso sounds of the country's best-known band, Dimension Costena, while Dantos was spurred on by its trumpet players. None of the fans was unaware of the political realities surrounding baseball. A few years before, when the national team was doing poorly in a Cuban tournament, *La Prensa* (the opposition paper) called for the manager's removal. President Daniel Ortega telephoned the manager to assure him that his post was secure. Not long after, *La Prensa* was banned for its opposition to Ortega, but many a big-league official must have wished a similar fate on his own home-town critics.

Attempting to stir up American public opinion against the Sandinistas, White House operative Oliver North told "N.B.C. Nightly News" commentator Tom Brokaw that he had evidence of a Cuban buildup in the Central American nation. Pointing to an aerial photograph of a Nicaraguan baseball diamond, he said, "Nicaraguans don't play baseball, but Cubans do." (Such a sabre-rattling technique would have surprised Baltimore and later Montreal pitcher Dennis Martinez, from Nicaragua, whose major-league career dated back to 1976.)

Before the final game, the Dantos batboy cast black-magic spells on the bases; their efficacy was proved when Costenos made six errors in the second inning, allowing six runs, and Dantos reliever Elvin Jarquin held Costenos to three hits in five innings as his team romped to a relatively easy 11–4 victory.

Most acknowledge that the level of Nicaraguan baseball has suffered since the end of the nation's normal relations with the United States. A similar fate awaited the Cubans after Castro came to power in the late 1950s, but thirty years later, the island nation is the number-one amateur power in the world.

Cuba had produced many players with major-league potential in the first half of the century. A lot of them, such as pitcher José Méndez, were black, and therefore not welcome in the big leagues. In 1911, Cincinnati signed two Cubans, Armando Marsans and Rafael Almeida, after "verifying" that they were pure Caucasian, a credential most Cubans must have scoffed at. Perhaps the greatest player was Martin Dihigo, who debuted as a shortstop in 1923. He was called the black Babe Ruth because of his superlative hitting and pitching skills and, in 1938, he led the Mexican League with a .387 batting average, an 18–2 pitching record, and an ERA of 0.90. Another black Cuban, Silvio Garcia, lost an opportunity to join the Brooklyn Dodgers after the war, when in response to Branch Rickey's question of what he would do if a white American slapped him, he replied, "I kill him." Instead, Garcia played several seasons in the outlaw Quebec Provincial League.

Cuba was a popular stopping point for American ball teams in those days. In the early 1940s, the Brooklyn Dodgers trained there in the spring, and spent their evenings drinking and fighting (particularly their erratic reliever Hugh Casey) with Ernest Hemingway.

By the 1950s, however, black Cubans, such as Sandy Amoros and Minnie Minoso, were joining major-league rosters; in 1954, the Havana Sugar Kings joined the International League, the top-rated minor association. Cuba was an open country in which gambling and organized crime reigned under the corrupt dictatorship of Fulgencio Batista. Martin Dihigo was a political exile living in Mexico, where he gave financial support to Che Guevera and later to the Granma expedition, which launched Fidel Castro's overthrow of Batista. Castro himself was a former pitcher at the University of Havana and was once scouted by the Washington Senators. In coming to power, despite his communist sympathies, he proved to be the game's greatest supporter. In 1959, he was among those who watched as the Sugar Kings won the Little World Series of minor-league baseball over a team from Minneapolis. Castro would arrive in a bullet-proof car that entered through the centre-field gates and drove him to his box seat. During a regular-season game with Rochester, however, a third-base coach for the visiting Americans was winged in the shoulder by a bullet from a celebrating revolutionary outside the stadium. Midway through the 1960 season, as relations between Cuba and the United States ruptured, the team's franchise was moved to Jersey City, and the last generation of Cubans to play in the major leagues—including Tony Oliva, Luis Tiant, Bert Campaneris, and Tony Perez—left the country.

Cut off from the American supply of baseball equipment, Cubans began to make their own. Gradually, they rebuilt their playing rosters. The two countries' amateur teams were evenly matched in the 1960s, but Bert Hooton's 1970 no-hitter over the Cubans was the last major American victory for some time.

As is true anywhere, in Cuba the home team is supported and the umpires are booed. However, Cuban fans, who sip strong cups of coffee throughout the game, return balls hit into the stands.

Cuba stands supreme among the amateur powers of baseball, and her star players profess only admiration for their country's system. "The love of my countrymen means more to me than dollars," said Pedro Jose Rodriguez in 1980, "and if anyone is dreaming that I would go to the big leagues, they should wake up."

It is easy to dismiss such sentiments as those of a player who really has

Baseball classes for Israeli youth at the American Zionist House in Tel Aviv, 1962.

no choice, but there is no question that most Latin ballplayers are far more comfortable at home. On the nearby island that the Dominican Republic shares with Haiti, baseball has flourished since the dictator Trujillo welcomed black stars in the 1930s. Today, the Dominican lives off sugar cane, tourism, and the export of talented ballplayers, one of whom, George Bell, was the American League's most valuable player in 1987. Although the Dominican Republic is not rich, its star players return each winter from the truly foreign land of North America.

Baseball was introduced to Venezuela by warships that docked there in the late nineteenth century. Far from resenting these developments, the locals were soon converted. "Venezuela never felt that beisbol was imported," said sportswriter Rudolfo Marniello. "We felt like it was created here. When Richard Nixon visited Caracas, the students threw rocks at him and shouted, 'Yanqui, go home!', but these same students came to the stadium and never shouted, 'Yankee, go home!'"

Ballparks throb with the sounds of salsa, the chorus of shouting, hand-clapping spectators dancing to the pounding of the *tambores* (five-foot-long drums made of the boles of avocado trees), and the cries of gamblers wagering on each pitch. The smell of the *criollas*, fried *platanos*, and *conya de quesa* hawked by Mestizo women and of the cold beer sold by an army of vendors fills the parks.

Venezuela's major-league graduates include Hall of Famer Luis Aparicio and, more recently, Montreal's rising star Andres Galarraga, but most doubt that this country will match the Dominican's record; said one observer, "Dominican players are just plain hungrier. It's much more prosperous here."

In the Far East, the game's tradition meshes with local custom. Korea and Taiwan have both become respectable outposts. In fact, Taiwan wins the Little League title in Williamsport, Pennsylvania (players must be twelve and under at the start of the season), with such regularity that one American in 1973 accused the island nation of using midgets hired by Chiang Kai-Shek to humiliate the United States.

Baseball was first introduced to Taiwan by the Japanese, who occupied the island from 1895 to 1945. Taiwanese-born but Japanese-educated adults such as Hsieh Kuo-cheng, who played right field for a Taiwanese primary-school team in the 1930s before attending Japan's Waseda University, organized the Taiwan Baseball Association in 1948, at a time when all but four of the diamonds on the island had been ploughed up to grow crops during the war.

For twenty years, the Taiwanese kept the game alive despite the cool interest shown by the mainland Chinese, who took Japan's place after the war. Rubber balls were used in place of expensive hardballs, but Taiwan nevertheless won its first little-league title in Pennsylvania in 1969.

No country has embraced baseball with as much tenacity and cultural creativity as the Japanese. The game was already well established at the start of the Second World War, and the Americans who flew on General Jimmy Doolittle's 1942 bombing raid over Tokyo reported feelings of guilt brought on by the sight of children below playing baseball on makeshift sandlot diamonds.

The game retained its amateur status within Japan's school system well into the 1930s. Not that North American influence had not been felt: both collegiate and professional teams from North America had toured there right after the First World War. Among them were a Japanese-Canadian club, the Asahis of Vancouver, and a Japanese-American team from Seattle, who spent fourteen days on the Pacific Ocean in 1921 to play Japanese students in a country many of them had never seen before.

It was two visits by major-league stars in the 1930s that changed the face of the Japanese game. In 1931, Matsutaro Shoriki, owner and publisher of the *Yomiuri Shimbun* newspaper, invited an all-star team that included Lou Gehrig, Charlie Gehringer, Al Simmons, and Lefty Grove. Three years later, an even more glorious tour was led by Babe Ruth. Both touring teams went undefeated but, in 1934, a nineteen-year-old Japanese pitcher, Eji Sawamura, struck out Gehringer, Ruth, Jimmie Foxx, and Gehrig, all in a row. Shoriki was impressed with the possibilities of native athletes and, acting on the advice of American professional Lefty O'Doul, formed the professional Yomiuri Giants in late 1934. In the next couple of years, the Hanshin Tigers of Osaka (owned by a railroad company), the Chunichi Dragons of Magoya (newspapers), and the Hankyu Braves of Nishinomiya (railroad) were established and joined in Japan's first fully professional baseball league (later called the Central League) in 1936. The Nankai Hawks of Osaka (railroad) joined them two years later.

By the time of the Second World War, players were seen as samurais or knights, loyal to their overlord in a kind of feudal hierarchy. The strongest curse a Japanese soldier could launch at his American counterpart was "Death to Babe Ruth".

Among the first Americans to play in Japan after the war was Phil Paine, a Boston Braves pitcher, who suited up in 1953 while serving with the United States Air Force. The Chunichi Dragons, however, took the first significant steps to import American stars when they brought in Don

The Italian team at the 1984 Summer Olympics in Los Angeles.

Newcombe and Larry Doby in 1962. Both played poorly and thus began the love-hate relationship between visiting Americans and their Japanese hosts.

The problem has been twofold. American players often arrived in Japan either at the end of their careers or because their unruly temperaments had exhausted the patience of their former employers.

Outrageous behaviour, however, is not respected in Japan, where players are expected to conform to team discipline and harmony, or *wa*. A moody or bitter ballplayer who disrupted this system would be blamed for any losing streaks, no matter how well he played.

In addition, the Japanese were slower in changing their game when the longball came into use after the war. Before the war, the smaller Japanese player compensated for his lack of power (even though distances down the line of 300 feet and 390 feet to centre are considerably shorter than those in American parks) by developing the principles of inside baseball. As a result, to this day power hitters are called on to bunt with a runner on base even when the element of surprise has long departed. Infielders will play in to cut off a run at home plate even in the first inning. The big inning is less feared than allowing the other team to gain the upper hand of a one-run lead.

Sadaharu Oh, Japan's greatest player, surpassed Hank Aaron's North American home-run record in 1977.

While the relation of the player to his team has been slow to take on North American characteristics, the game on the field has changed since the war. In 1964, for instance, an American, Daryl Spencer, introduced the take-out at second base. Previously, on a double-play ball, the runner going to second meekly strode off the base line if it looked as though he would be retired. Spencer, however, slid hard, upending the second baseman, and soon his teammates adopted the style. A few years later, Masanori Murakami, the first Japanese to play in the American major leagues (with San Francisco in 1964–65), threw what was reported to be the first brushback pitch.

Perhaps the greatest change, however, was in the players' physical stature. Victor Starfin, a Russian born on the northern island of Hokkaido, was an early pitching star for the Yomiuri Giants. At 6' 4", 230 pounds, he overwhelmed his more diminutive teammates. Another big and strong Japanese, Michio Nishizawa, pounded out 212 home runs before retiring in 1958.

The player who truly changed Japanese baseball's self-image was born in Tokyo on May 20, 1940, to a Japanese mother and Chinese father. With front leg poised heron-like, and bat, sometimes touching his helmet, tilted back over his head towards the pitcher, Sadaharu Oh became the world's greatest home-run hitter on September 3, 1977, when he surpassed Henry Aaron's record of 755. ("The mental pressure was so great, it was almost physical," Oh said.) Oh proved that the Japanese could hit for power and thereby helped banish the old emphasis on pitching.

He did it by following the precepts of his mentor or *sensei,* Hiroshi Arakawa. They met when Oh was a fourteen-year-old sandlot player. Arakawa had hoped to steer him to the Waseda Business School, and believed that by applying the principles of Zen and *bushido* to the bat (or sword), he could transform Oh into a great slugger. From *aiki-do,* the martial art combining judo, karate, and Zen, he taught Oh the one-legged, Mel Ott style of batting in which the first leg is raised during the act of hitting. "The style," Arakawa said mysteriously, "permits him to concentrate better." In practice, Oh would balance on one leg for three minutes.

Philosophically, the teacher wanted his pupil to achieve a spiritual oneness with his art, to eliminate the *ma,* or space, between the batter and pitcher. Success was achieved by developing inner strength rather than outer muscle. "My baseball career," Oh concluded, "was a long, long initiation into a single secret: that at the heart of all things is love."

In the end, Oh hit 868 home runs before retiring in 1980. He was the Babe Ruth to a series of equally marvellous ballplayers, including the Lou Gehrig–like Isao Harimoto, whose Korean heritage was looked down upon by the Japanese (players will often bait umpires by crying, "You lousy Korean!"). Harimoto hit .383 for the Nippon Ham Fighters (owned by a meat-packing company) and won six Pacific League batting titles before being traded to the Giants. Another supporting actor, Shigeo Nagashima, won six Central League batting titles but is remembered best for hitting the game-winning home run (or "sayonara") in the first professional game attended by Emperor Hirohito.

In many ways, the Japanese game remains a mystery to outsiders. An established manager may be sent on *kyuyo* (Japanese for "rest" or "recuperation") rather than being fired. Sometimes this practice saves face for a manager, allowing him to resign; at other times, it is a legitimate tactic aimed at correcting a team member's bad habits and forcing him to take responsibility for what happens on the field. For the Japanese, the team is less a corporation in the American sense (though all are controlled by large businesses) than an extended family in which the errors of one member reflect on the others. To demand more money is unacceptable because it suggests the player has put his interests ahead of all others'. Only foreigners, or *gaijin*, such as Bob Horner, therefore have the luxury of demanding enormous pay.

Japanese teams train and live together for ten months and such communal exercises as daily ten-mile runs or the "Death Climb" of the Taiyo Whales (owned by a fishery), in which the players do 20 sprints up and down the 275 steps of a Shinto shrine, are not extraordinary.

Ballparks, on the other hand, seldom reflect the order and ritual of Japanese tradition. From the visitor's perspective the riot of colour in the dense display of banner ads with their Japanese lettering creates a bizarre otherworldly effect. Flags, whistles, drums, trumpets, and trombones, played by supporters in brilliantly coloured *happi* coats, begin their blaring encouragement as the home team comes to bat and continue relentlessly through to the end of the game.

Whisky, sake, and beer from Japan's four major breweries are sold along with dishes as varied as sushi, squid, fish cakes, and hot dogs. Ticket prices range from $2.25 (U.S.) for bleacher seats to $30 behind home plate, but games at stadiums such as the Giants' Korakuen are usually virtual sell-outs. In 1984, nearly three million fans attended the Giants' sixty-five home games. The completely enclosed stadium is double-decked and the superb electronic scoreboard shows replays, as is done in any American park. Sophisticated public-transit systems obviate the need for vast parking lots near Japanese parks: Chunichi's Nagoya Stadium is served by a 130 mile-per-hour bullet train that whizzes by behind the left-field fence.

Just how good is Japanese baseball? Such questions reflect a somewhat obsessive need to compare and tend to ignore the relative and contextual nature of one person's ability in relation to another's. Various observations can be made: Takeido Kaku, a Taiwanese-born player, had his pitch clocked at ninety-seven miles per hour in 1985; the players are in wonderful shape as a result of eight to fifteen-hour days of actual play and exercise; the game strategies of Japanese baseball often deny the opportunity for a dramatic expression of the individual player's ability; the Kansas City Royals managed only a 9–7–1 split during their 1981 tour. It is interesting to note, however, that no one questions the standard of play in the American major leagues when a player stars with one team after having failed with his previous team, but should he jump to Japan and outshine his former performance, analysts dismiss the change as apparent only in the context of the weaker Japanese game.

There is no ultimate resolution in this debate. At the level of twelve-year-olds, the skill of Taiwanese lads surpasses that of any other little-league player in the world. At the amateur college level, the Japanese proved by their victory in the 1984 Olympics that an American lineup of players as strong as Will Clark, Mark McGwire, B.J. Surhoff, Cory Snyder, and Mike Dunne was not unbeatable. And, while a true world series may not be possible until well into the next century, we can agree that the game's world-wide expansion has finally realized, at least in part, Al Spalding's hundred-year-old dream.

CHEERING FOR THE HOME TEAM

INNING
9

In the last century, professional baseball became elevated from pure recreation to a kind of heightened experience of everyday life. Here were men who could perform wonderful acts for a living—the shamans and witchdoctors of the distant past had been replaced by ballplayers. In many arts where folk tradition has taken on the character of commercial entertainment, the public's willingness to participate is limited to spectatorship. And while this is to some extent true of baseball, the passive role is not as readily accepted, perhaps because of the rootedness and universality of the game.

The attempt to connect private lives to the great public theatre of organized baseball has spawned a growth industry of collectibles, among which the autograph and the baseball card are the most sought-after examples. As well, a library of books and films has been produced to help redefine the public's image of the game. Just as Jim Bouton's *Ball Four* gave us the first mature look at real ballplayers, so Roger Kahn's *Boys of Summer* reminded us of the magical hold the past retains on today's game.

There are moments in the history of autograph collecting that demonstrate the strange—and sometimes macabre—ways in which ballplayers can gain a kind of immortality. Fritz Coumbe acquired a rather ordinary 38–58 pitching record between 1914 and 1921, but he is remembered best for dying in 1978, while signing a 3" by 5" card much sought-after by hobby collectors. The card belonged to John Goldberg, a professor in the Department of Foreign Languages at West Virginia University, who recalled: "He went into a coma while signing and never recovered. You can see where he tails off at the end of the signature. His daughter sent me a very nice letter. She said that even though her father was very sick, he insisted on signing my item."

Serious autograph collecting begins with Babe Ruth. Since he made himself accessible and signed everything, the value of his autograph has little to do with rarity and much to do with magic.

The autograph is a kind of talisman whose power lies in its authenticity. A copy or a forgery is worthless, since what is prized is the second or two of the big-league player's time captured in his signature. Possess that signature and you are a part of that moment of history. (For that reason, the habit of certain ballplayers, such as Herm Winningham, a Montreal Expo, and Barry Latman, who played with five major-league teams from 1957 to 1967, of rubber-stamping rather than signing baseball cards mailed to them is particularly vexing to the collector.)

Opposite: Intrepid spectators seeking a better view at Boston's Huntington Avenue Grounds during the 1903 World Series.

Members of the 1952 Brooklyn Dodgers, as immortalized on Topps baseball cards.

There was a time when autograph hunting was largely the sport of children, but the growth in the value of collectibles has made an industry of the hobby. And while a rubber-stamped signature can be rather like a slap in the face, it is less depressing than the charmless North American practice of having present and past major-leaguers sell their autographs at collecting shows.

Willie Mays has become a dour attendee of these paid signing sessions, where, with head bowed and pen at the ready, he churns out a dizzying supply of instant memories for eager recipients who babble on about how much his great catch in the 1954 World Series meant to them and are met with only an icy stare or, more often, the top of Mays's balding head as they move along the autograph assembly line.

Joe DiMaggio charges $18,000 for a day of autograph signing (and will not sign Hall of Fame bats because they are immediately resold for several hundred dollars); Ted Williams demands $5,000 per hour; and Mickey Mantle, $10 per signature. Once again, money has displaced the magic.

Dan Petry of the 1988 California Angels rejected autograph shows because, "I couldn't look a little kid in the eye knowing he had paid two or three dollars for my autograph." Rare, however, is the present-day ball-player (Minnesota's John Moses is one) who will take time during batting practice to walk over to sign autographs for a line of eager fans. These John Moses collectors did not care that his career average at the end of 1987 was .248 with seven home runs, but they did care about baseball and about being a part of it.

Baseball cards date back to the successful use of lithography to reproduce photographs inexpensively. In the 1880s, ballplayers wore pop-eyed expressions from the violent discharge of flash required to light the studios in which they pretended to catch fly balls suspended by string from the ceiling. Old Judge Cigarettes were among the first to put cards in their packages—clearly, the audience was not originally children. (Nor is it now. In 1910, Honus Wagner, the bowlegged shortstop of the Pittsburgh Pirates from 1900 to 1917 and a non-smoker, threatened to sue the manufacturer of Sweet Caporal cigarettes when it used his picture on one of their cards. Perhaps only two dozen cards were printed before production was suspended and those that leaked out have become prized by collec-

tors. Offers as high as $50,000 have been made for originals.)

Throughout the first three decades of the twentieth century, other companies, such as *The Sporting Life* newspaper, Tip Top Bread, and Cracker Jack, occasionally issued cards in series, but it was the packaging of cards with bubble gum in the 1930s by the Goudey Company of Boston that launched the modern era of baseball cards. There was a hiatus in production during the Second World War, but by the late 1940s and early 1950s, Leaf and Bowman and then Topps (whose first major set appeared in 1951) realized commercial success.

The Mickey Mantle card of 1952 issued by Topps, a Brooklyn confectionery firm, was purchased at a Toronto auction in 1981 for $900. By the end of the decade, it had appreciated in value tenfold. Topps issued 407 cards in 1952, but of the four series issued, the last one—numbers 311 to 407—received only limited distribution. Mantle made his first Topps appearance as number 311.

Topps remained the undisputed leader in the production of baseball cards for almost three decades until companies such as Donruss and Fleer went after the burgeoning collectors' market that emerged in the 1980s and, more than anything else, ensured that Mickey Mantle's card would be a strong hedge against inflation.

Just as baseball-card collecting has reached a level of commercial maturity that leaves the sentimentalist chagrined at another loss for childhood, so has the motion-picture industry recognized the box-office draw of the national pastime.

Commenting on Joe DiMaggio's divorce from Marilyn Monroe in 1955, Oscar Levant acidly noted, "It proves no man can be a success in two national pastimes." The attempt to create a successful marriage between baseball and the movies has often left both parties unhappy: documentaries are hobbled by a narrow literalness and feature films ride off in all directions on the sentimental aspects of the game.

Ernest Thayer's poem "Casey at the Bat" was set to music, then staged as opera, and was filmed for the first time in 1899. Paramount released its version in 1927, with Wallace Beery as the tragic slugger whose downfall was a combination of pride and one too many drinks. Thomas Edison's *How the Office Boy Saw the Ball Game*, released in 1906, is generally acknowledged as the first commercial film in which baseball is a significant

Premier issue of Sports Illustrated, *August 16, 1954.*

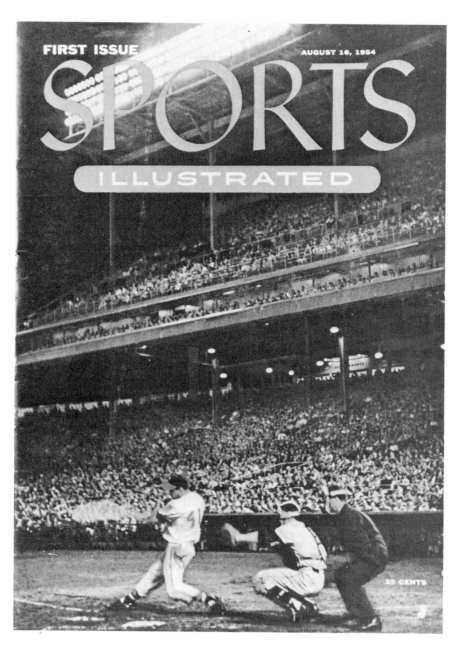

part of the story line. Movie patrons laughed at the exploits of an office clerk who takes off from work to attend a game and finds his boss in the next seat. (A year later, *How Jones Saw the Ball Game* recycled the plot.)

The public's appetite for baseball scenes grew with the sophistication of movie production. A spring-training game between the Giants and the St. Louis Browns was recorded in 1925 by a motion-picture company hoping to capitalize on the Florida real-estate boom and the expanding circuit of clubs in training. The only detectable plot was the one behind the filming. In the eighth inning, with the Browns in the field, the game was stopped and cameras were placed in back of first, third, and the pitcher's mound. The hero, who looked as though he had never held a bat, let alone swung one, flailed it at an imaginary ball and then raced round the bases.

The director called for a retake. "If he has to go around the bases again, he'll either fall down or throw up," Giants manager McGraw told a nearby reporter. Sure enough, the hero made imaginary contact, then stumbled around the bases, just managing to cross the plate before he was sick.

"I never saw a well-trained ballplayer who could run around the bases at top speed twice without a rest in between. So what chance did that poor ham have to do it?" McGraw remarked later.

Ring Lardner's *Alibi Ike,* released by Warner Brothers in 1935 and starring Joe E. Brown and nineteen-year-old Olivia de Havilland, was one of the first full-scale feature-length baseball films. The story concerns a rookie with natural pitching and hitting skills and an unnatural ability to find an excuse for every pitfall he encounters.

Baseball's cinema success story of the age, however, was *The Pride of the Yankees* (RKO, 1942), with Gary Cooper as the tragic Lou Gehrig, a great athlete destroyed by a terrifying disease. Cooper's delivery of Gehrig's farewell address to 60,000 fans in Yankee Stadium caught the hearts of the 1942 audience facing the inevitable tragedy of the Second World War.

The story of the Yankees' other great star, Babe Ruth (released in 1948, with William Bendix playing Ruth as a kind of blundering, big-hearted oaf), has roundly been labelled the worst of the genre. Except for the most superficial of details (for example, Ruth's 60 home runs in 1927), the film makes no effort to be accurate and is ultimately successful only as a simple baseball story for children.

Two other film biographies of the period were really nothing more than moral tales. Grover Cleveland Alexander, played by Ronald Reagan (*The*

Named to the Hall of Fame in 1955, Joe DiMaggio is best known today for his coffee commercials and attendance at old-timer reunions where his is the most eagerly sought autograph.

The legendary Shoeless Joe Jackson was banned from baseball for his role in fixing the 1919 World Series. Despite a lifetime batting average of .356 (third-best all-time, behind Ty Cobb at .367 and Rogers Hornsby at .358) he remains excluded from baseball's Hall of Fame.

Winning Team, released by Warner Brothers in 1952) and Dizzy Dean, portrayed by Dan Dailey (*The Pride of St. Louis,* Twentieth Century Fox, also in 1952) are shown as likeable rubes whose careers are threatened by the bottle but who are redeemed by the loving, stalwart missus, allowing our heroes to make splendid comebacks.

Some films used fantasy to capture the romance of the game. In *It Happens Every Spring* (Twentieth Century Fox, 1949), a compound that makes a ball avoid wood allows the hero (played by Ray Milland) to perfect a knuckleball-type throw that carries his team to the championship. *Angels in the Outfield* (MGM, 1951) casts Paul Douglas as the gruff, rather unpleasant manager of a Pittsburgh team led to victory by angels behind each of his players. Robert Redford's *The Natural* (Tri-Star, 1984) continued the tradition of fantasy, using the hero's bat, Wonderboy, and a climactic scene in which Roy Hobbs's home run produces celestial results. The film was attacked by some for being unfaithful to the book, but critics seemed to forget that the author of the book, Bernard Malamud, had also taken fictional liberties with the real-life shooting of Eddie Waitkus, the Philadel-

Left to right: Arnold "Chick" Gandil (played by Michael Rooker), Fred McMullin (played by Perry Lang), Charles "Swede" Risberg (played by Don Harvey), and Oscar "Hap" Felsch (played by Charlie Sheen) in Eight Men Out, *the story of the fixing of the 1919 World Series, a critically acclaimed movie released in 1988.*

phia Phillie who was gunned down by an unbalanced admirer, Ruth Ann Steinhagen, at the start of the 1949 season, but recovered to play six more big-league seasons.

The ability of Malamud's book to successfully capture the magic and the reality of baseball had led many filmmakers to consider the possibilities of the theme. Until *The Natural*, the results had not always been commercially successful. *Bang the Drum Slowly* (Paramount, 1973) starred Robert de Niro as a baseball rube dying of Hodgkin's Disease and was a critical success with little box-office fire, despite the marvellous performance of Vincent Gardenia as a Tom Lasorda look-alike.

Bull Durham and *Eight Men Out*, released in 1988, took screen baseball into the realm of realism through the magic of film. *Bull Durham* gave us a racy, somewhat uninhibited view of baseball at the minor-league level, an aspect of the game rarely depicted on the screen. *Eight Men Out* documented dramatically the throwing of the 1919 World Series, and in so doing faced the ultimate challenge of the baseball movie—to make the action on a fictional diamond seem as real to us as what we know and love about the real. The film's success was a testament to how well that complex challenge was met.

Early documentary films about baseball tended to be quite literal. However, since most fans were intrigued by any moving images of their favourite stars, these rather wooden efforts had some measure of success. *Christy Mathewson and the New York National League Team* was released in 1907, and one of the first World Series films featured the 1910 Philadelphia Athletics–Chicago Cubs matchup. October 17 was a cold day, and Athletics manager Connie Mack was in an even frostier mood over the delay caused by the presence of cameramen on the field in Philadelphia's Shibe

Bud Abbott and Lou Costello immortalized the "Who's on First" routine in which the hapless Lou also learns that "what's" on second and "I don't know" is on third.

Park. Umpire Hank O'Day ordered the crew back into the stands but, in perhaps one of the first examples of the media's power to dictate to baseball officials, the filmmakers angrily demanded that American League president Ban Johnson allow them to stay, as promised. Johnson called over another ump, Tom Connolly, and announced that the cameramen could remain. Then Cub manager Frank Chance balked at their presence behind home plate.

Mack was furious because his pitcher, Chief Bender, who had already warmed up, was starting to tighten up; none the less, once the cameramen were in place, Bender pitched a three-hitter and the Athletics took the first game on their way to a 4–1 series victory.

With the advent of talkies in the 1930s, the major leagues began to market their game aggressively by providing high-quality films for use at no cost by civic groups. Lew Fonseca, one-time American League batting champion (.369 in 1929) and Chicago White Sox manager (1932–34), put his own filmmmaking hobby to work by producing a series of instructional films for his players, and thereby became a pioneer in what field managers now take for granted. By the 1940s, Fonseca's footage of training camp, all-star games, and World Series matches were the instant replays of the day, helping to fill out many movie-theatre double bills.

Fonseca's baseball films of the 1940s and 1950s were soon part of the game's visual vernacular. A close-up of a World Series hero was jump cut with footage of a series highlight involving that player and the crowd, in

unison, rising to cheer him. The viewer is to believe, for example, that a
Yogi Berra home run in Ebbets Field touched off jubilation among
Brooklyn fans or that Yankee Stadium erupted in cheers in 1955 when
Sandy Amoros caught Berra's long drive in the seventh game of the series.
Images such as those of Thomson's home run in 1951 or Mays's catch off
Wertz in 1954 were, by dint of sheer repetition, drummed into the collec-
tive unconscious of an entire nation.

Technological improvement did not change the format of this kind of
visual until the advent of pay television and videotaping. Insofar as a
Philadelphia television station's contribution of $600,000 to the free-agent
signing of Pete Rose by the Phillies in 1979 consummated baseball's longstanding affair with the media, imaginative baseball documentary filming
has cemented that relationship at the artistic level. Pay television made
popular the three-minute rock video, and baseball preview films of the
1980s showed a willingness to experiment with new styles of music and
different images of the game. The collaboration of director John Sayles and
production designer Nora Chavooshian on *Eight Men Out* was a natural
outgrowth of their work on the baseball-inspired Bruce Springsteen rock
video "Glory Days". Videotaping opened up a new market for baseball
films, such as *The Boys of Summer* (VidAmerica, 1983), based on Roger
Kahn's bestseller of the early 1970s. With an additional decade of material
to supplement Kahn's work, the video paints a poignant portrait of the
passing of time for the much-storied Brooklyn Dodgers of the early 1950s.
Sid Caesar's commentary substitutes a fan's voice for the sportswriter's.
The video *Heroes to Heartaches: Boston Sports since 1975* (Phoenix Communi-
catons, 1987) depicts with almost horrific detail a succession of close Red
Sox seasons from 1975 to the team's awesome undoing in 1986, one out
from World Series victory.

It is a testament to baseball's attraction that some popular artistic efforts
that would almost certainly have been long forgotten had they been born
of nostalgia for almost anything else, live on.

Jack Norworth saw his first baseball games as a fan cheering for the
Brooklyn Dodgers on their way to the 1916 National League pennant.
Nothing odd about that, except that eight years previously, while riding
the new New York City subway, he had been inspired by an ad for a
ballgame at the Polo Grounds to pen the classic song, "Take Me Out to the
Ball Game". Norworth's unabashed boosterism ("Let's root root root for
the home team...if they don't win it's a shame") became an American
standard at once (Norworth was unable to use it in his own vaudeville act
because every performer ahead of him on the bill was using it as well).

"Jolting Joe DiMaggio" and "I Love Mickey" in the 1950s, Simon and
Garfunkel's "Mrs. Robinson" ("Where have you gone, Joe DiMaggio?") in
the late 1960s, John Fogerty's "Centerfield" and Terry Cashman's "Talkin'
Baseball" in the 1980s have come (and gone) but none works quite as well
or has as much fan appeal as the endearing seventh-inning-stretch sounds
of Norworth's tune.

The hundredth anniversary of DeWolf Hopper's delivery of Ernest L.
Thayer's "Casey at the Bat" in New York's Wallach's Theatre was marked
in 1988. Thayer, a Harvard philosopher, found the success of the poem
that he had tossed off for a column in the *San Francisco Examiner* confound-
ing. Yet, one hundred years later, Glenn Stout would state unequivocally
in *The SABR Review of Books: A Forum of Baseball Literary Opinion* that
"Casey at the Bat" remains the most memorable piece of baseball writing
ever produced, and *Sports Illustrated* would honour the anniversary with
an article on the events leading up to Casey's at-bat. From the ominous
opening—"The outlook wasn't brilliant for the Mudville nine that day"—

Bob Uecker, Cardinals catcher, plays the tuba prior to the second game of the 1964 World Series. Uecker's reputation for zaniness was enhanced after his playing career by his appearance in a series of beer commercials and his role as a play-by-play broadcaster for the Milwaukee Brewers.

*"The game isn't over 'til it's over"
and "You've got to be very careful if
you don't know where you are going
because you might not get there"—
Yogi Berra's mots have made him
the game's most beloved sage.*

to the dramatic closing—"But there is no joy in Mudville—Mighty Casey had struck out"—the poem captures the timeless confrontation of batter and pitcher and the frustrated dreams of hometown fans.

The "Mudville nine" were a symbol of the frenzied popularity of baseball in the nineteenth century, but the twentieth belongs to the Brooklyn Dodgers. Even the name has resonance, conjuring the lilt of an Irish folk tune and the rasp of the Dead-End Kids. As much as the name speaks of tradition, it speaks out of memory: the fabled team ceased to be, following the 1957 season. The Dodgers' transfer to Los Angeles, like that of the motion-picture industry a half century earlier, was part of a large national shift in aspiration that looked west and saw there, flourishing in a perennially benign environment of beaches, suntans, and movie stars, a level of success unattainable elsewhere.

Brooklyn fans might have seen that the Dodgers were living on borrowed time as early as 1954 when Dodger owner Walter O'Malley got rid of Red Barber, who had delighted a generation of Brooklyn fans with his colourful descriptions of "rhubarbs" in the "catbird seat" and bases that were "COD—chock full of Dodgers", and replaced him with Andre Baruch, whose imaginative leaps extended only so far as to have runners sliding into second base standing up. However, Baruch was married to Bea Wain, a glamorous singer of the day, and O'Malley was a man deeply impressed by showbiz. In that respect, the parochial Brooklyn lawyer was probably no different from legions of his fellow residents. When he took the Dodgers from Brooklyn, he was merely realizing the borough dream.

There are, of course, many reasons offered to explain the Dodgers' transfer, ranging from the promise of three hundred acres of land in Los Angeles, through guaranteed profits from pay television, to the freedom to operate in a market bereft of major-league competition.

Brooklyn, which had become part of metropolitan New York in 1898, was a reason in itself. The borough was in decline: its newspaper, *The Eagle,* had folded; its transit line, the El, had disappeared; its more affluent residents had fled to Long Island; and the spirit that had inspired Brooklyn to lead the nation by having the first integrated ball team had disappeared under the weight of hostility shown by its established white population to the increasing numbers of blacks in the borough.

Racial tensions followed fans to the ballpark and then kept them at home. Where the team had drawn over 1.8 million in the late 1940s, the crowds had declined by more than half a million by the 1950s; in 1955, the year the Dodgers won the World Series, attendance barely creeped over a million. The exuberant supporters of the late 1940s who had responded to the rooting musical leadership of the Dodger Symphony and the clanging bell of Hilda Chester were now more sullen and less forgiving of a team that provided only seven hundred parking spaces. Suburban fans preferred to stay home and watch the games on television.

Brooklyn was politically outfoxed by the boosterism of Los Angeles, which began to court O'Malley seriously in 1955. In New York, the last-minute intervention by Nelson Rockefeller was no match for the city's real civic power broker, Robert Moses, who opposed dedication of land upon which a stadium would be built and owned by the ballclubs. Los Angeles politicians, despite a small but determined opposition who picketed City Hall with placards proclaiming "Save Chavez Ravine", were willing to use Title 1 of the Federal Housing Act of 1949, which was designed to eliminate urban slums by selling land to a private developer "whose construction would conform to a larger public purpose".

Rockefeller declared that "the city should be a little more aware of the factors which make it great. We've got to stop taking them for granted; we can't expect them to be here forever if we do."

There were protests in New York, but the mayor's secretary noted that only "an occasional letter dribbles in." Some columnists pointed out that the ten-year subway series that pitted either the Giants or the Dodgers against the Yankees was becoming a tad tiresome. Robert Creamer of *Sports Illustrated* seemed to speak for everyone: "the most cheerful aspect of the Dodgers' imminent transfer to Los Angeles is that at long last (and about time) the New York Yankee–Brooklyn Dodger World Series routine is over, done with, finished, as dead as vaudeville."

When the Dodgers left Brooklyn, Sid Caesar related in the video *Boys of Summer* twenty-five years later, an era ended but a legend began. That legend has become more powerful than the team that inspired it, making the Brooklyn Dodgers a metaphor for the public meaning of baseball.

The Dodgers carried the hopes of a nation in the postwar period. "Wait till next year!" was the Dodgers' theme, but they moved into the forefront

A twilight game at Ebbets Field.

by signing Jackie Robinson—a landmark in enlightenment in race relations. Underdog and champion—these roles have made Brooklyn the team of legend.

The Dodgers' legacy was fashioned before the Second World War. Prior to the 1934 season, Giants manager Bill Terry scornfully remarked, "Is Brooklyn still in the league?" On the last weekend of that season, those words would haunt him: the sixth-place Dodgers eliminated the Giants 5–1.

Brooklyn had been a baseball town as far back as 1849. The Atlantics, Excelsiors, Putnams, and Eckfords dominated the early game, the Eckfords starting the great Brooklyn–New York rivalry by defeating the Bronx's Unions of Morrisania 22–8 in 1856. Brooklyn joined a minor league in 1883; the next year, they entered the major-league American Association. When they joined the National League in 1890, they were known as the Bridegrooms—six of their players were newly married. Late in the nineteenth century, Charles Ebbets, who had started as an employee became part-owner of the team, and the driving force behind the building of the park named in his honour. Ground was broken on March 4, 1912,

Phil Rizzuto: the New York Yankee broadcaster is best known for his trademark call of "Holy Cow".

but to meet expenses, Ebbets had to sell 50 per cent of the club to the McKeever Brothers, prosperous Brooklyn contractors.

It is one of the ironies of the Brooklyn story that their showcase of baseball became their downfall. The tangled ownership years later brought the Brooklyn Trust Company into the play and, with it, Walter O'Malley.

Brooklyn's players had a certain panache that, in turn, gave character to the borough itself. From 1907 to 1916, Napoleon Rucker had a 2.42 earned-run average and a deceptive slow, slower, and slowest delivery; his 134 wins were equalled by his losses. Zack Wheat, an eventual Hall of Famer, played in Brooklyn from 1909 to 1926 and ended his career with a .317 batting average. Burleigh Grimes, another Hall of Famer and the last man to throw a legal spitball, expectorated in Brooklyn from 1918 to 1926 and won twenty or more games in four seasons. Yet despite two World Series appearances by the Dodgers in 1916 and 1920, they were only contenders until 1955. The late 1920s provided the "Flatbush faithful", as Dodger fans were now dubbed, with a lineup charitably renamed the "Daffiness Boys". The Dodgers were still managed by the corpulent and fading Wilbert (Uncle Robbie) Robinson, who had been hired in 1914. From 1922 to 1929, he led the Dodgers to seven sixth-place finishes.

A turn for the better followed the arrival in the late 1930s of Larry MacPhail and Branch Rickey. MacPhail had built a winning team in Cincinnati but had left under a cloud after a drunken punch-up with team owner Powell Crosley. The cloud was lifted, however, when he brought Hugh Casey, Dixie Walker, Pete Reiser, and Pee Wee Reese (the first of the boys of summer) to Brooklyn. In 1939, MacPhail hired a good shortstop (but a better gambler and street hustler), Leo Durocher, to manage the club. Durocher, like Billy Martin, antagonized a lot of people but redeemed himself with a pennant win in 1941.

The MacPhail–Durocher combination alarmed league authorities. Gamblers, bookmakers, and various underworld characters brought a shady sort of colour to the Brooklyn dressing room, but the team trained in Cuba where everything was allowed. (In one notorious incident in March 1942, a drinking bout involving several Dodgers and Ernest Hemingway ended in a boxing match between Hugh Casey and Hemingway, staged in the writer's living room. When Casey beat him, Hemingway challenged him to a duel—Casey's choice of weapon. It is ironic that these two troubled souls eventually took their own lives in a similar fashion some years later.)

After MacPhail left the Dodgers, Branch Rickey bought into the team and reformed it somewhat, before the war drained off the supply of able ballplayers.

The postwar era was a splendid one for Jackie Robinson and the Boys of Summer. In 1947, the World Series was televised and, within a few years, commentators were noting that rooftops once crammed with fans seeking an illegal view were now crowded with television antennas. By 1949, the Brooklyn organization's territorial map built up by Rickey looked like a successful general's campaign history. The Dodgers either owned outright or had close working agreements with twenty-seven teams, including Hollywood, Santa Barbara, and Medford up the Pacific Coast; Billings, Pueblo, Fort Worth, and Ponca City in the west; Miami, Mobile, and Valdosta in the south; Newport News, Geneva, and Pulaski in the northeast; and Montreal and Three Rivers in Canada.

The empire-building was an incredible enterprise but, ironically, its main beneficiary was Los Angeles, who would win five World Series titles to Brooklyn's one. That one, in 1955, sparked mass celebrations, but they came too late: fans looking back recall that their visits to Ebbets Field had been few and far between.

The sale of Ebbets Field in October 1956 for $3 million to a real-estate developer in many ways was the end of the Brooklyn Dodgers, even though they played one more season before departing. It was only in retrospect that many came to see that the Dodgers—the subject of thousands of street-corner conversations—had been the soul of the community.

Bill Reddy, a fan quoted in Peter Golenbock's *Bums*, recalled that O'Malley did "a terrible thing to the people of Brooklyn because he took away part of the cohesiveness that used to hold the borough together. Even if there was racial tension, at least they had something in common, something they could talk about." In Brooklyn baseball had been the common language that gave three million residents an identity, even though most outsiders saw only the one depicted by Hollywood—working class, somewhat sloppy, where every man had an ethnic last name and a penchant for chewing gum.

After Kahn's *The Boys of Summer* appeared, the Brooklyn Dodgers became a frame of reference for those eager to suggest that the new America of faceless office towers, jet-set lifestyles, and celebrity status was not such a wonderful thing after all. Brooklyn remains for many Americans an outpost in this shallow world, a place where all the best public and private values associated with baseball had once resided. In 1981, the longed-for richness of life in the past became the basis for action. As gentrification swept Brooklyn, creating a new urban landscape, New York State senator Thomas Bartosiewicz made what seemed to some an absurdly appropriate suggestion—why not return the Dodgers to Brooklyn?

On February 20, 1981, he wrote to Walter O'Malley's son Peter: "Mr. O'Malley, Brooklyn is making a tremendous comeback in the true Dodgers' tradition. That's why I introduced and passed a New York Senate Resolution expressing the hope that the Dodgers would return to their one and only true home, the County of Kings. Consideration of making the Dodgers the great Brooklyn Dodgers once again would be a monumental gesture on your part. It would symbolize the resurrection of the Great Northeast and stir the spirits of people who long for and dream about their team's return."

Perhaps the best known contemporary baseball personality, Billy Martin has had five turns as Yankee manager and awaits a sixth call.

Bartosiewicz went on to introduce a bill to set up a sports authority mandated to build what he called the "Ebbets Dome"; despite favourable publicity, it died in committee. In 1987, he was still apparently tilting at windmills, proposing to build a 17,000-seat stadium near the Coney Island Boardwalk to house a Triple-A franchise. Borough business leaders and politicians rallied in support and something of the old Brooklyn–New York rivalry was reborn. Interviewed about the project, New York Mets president Fred Wilpon said that a minor-league team "would infringe upon and take away from the Mets and Yankees; I don't think that's fair." What he was really objecting to may have been that a minor-league team would resurrect Brooklyn's interest in a major-league one. The legend of the Dodgers, benign in the abstract and relegated to the realm of cosy nostalgia, terrified major-league executives once it threatened to become a reality.

The Brooklyn Dodgers, who ceased to exist as a team in 1957, and their shrine, Ebbets Field, which was levelled in 1960 to make way for an apartment block, have in some ways gained strength in their demise as a kind of metaphor for the belief that baseball teams are ultimately public property. Continuing interest in the Dodgers shows that baseball is one of the supreme forms of private celebration in North America—that it touches us in deeply personal ways. We play catch with our parents on neighbourhood streets and they take us to the games where we cheer for our home team. And the idea begins to develop that a ball team is, at its root, a community enterprise. The Brooklyn Dodgers are the first team owned solely by their fans. That their players are at best middle-aged to senior citizens, or that their park is now an apartment complex matters not a wit. In Brooklyn, the fantasy has been adopted by players in the political arena and the results may fascinate, if not shake, baseball in the years ahead.

RECOMMENDED READING

Baseball may be the most analysed sport; pre-season reports, player and team biographies, scholarly studies, and novels featuring the game abound. Amassing a top-fifty list would be a daunting task, and what appears below makes no claims to be the fruits of that effort. Rather, these works, grouped by subject, are those to which I turned when I was writing this book and to which I would refer any reader with an interest in exploring further baseball's many dimensions.

An Overview of the Game

Boswell, Thomas. *How Life Imitates the World Series*. New York: Penguin Books, 1982.

———. *Why Time Begins on Opening Day*. New York: Penguin Books, 1984.

Bouton, Jim. *Ball Four*. Cleveland: World Publishing, 1970.

Gipe, George. *The Great American Sports Book*. New York: Doubleday, 1978.

Hall, Donald. *Fathers Playing Catch with Sons: Essays on Sport (Mostly Baseball)*. New York: Laurel, 1985.

Humber, William. *Cheering for the Home Team: The Story of Baseball in Canada*. Erin, Ont.: Boston Mills Press, 1983.

Kahn, Roger. *The Boys of Summer*. New York: Harper & Row, 1971.

Lieb, Fred. *Baseball as I Have Known It*. New York: Grosset & Dunlap, 1977.

Okrent, Daniel, and Levine, Harris. *The Ultimate Baseball Book*. Boston: Houghton Mifflin, 1981.

Ritter, Lawrence S. *The Glory of Their Times: The Story of the Early Days of Baseball Told by the Men Who Played It*. New York: Macmillan, 1966.

Baseball's Early Years

Adelman, Melvin L. *A Sporting Time: New York City and the Rise of Modern Athletics, 1820-70*. Chicago: University of Illinois Press, 1986.

Henderson, Robert W. *Ball, Bat and Bishop*. New York: Rockport Press, 1947.

Peterson, Harold. *The Man Who Invented Baseball*. New York: Scribner's, 1969.

Seymour, Harold. *Baseball*, 2 vols. New York: Oxford University Press, 1960, 1971.

Vincent, Ted. *Mudville's Revenge: The Rise and Fall of American Sport*. New York: Seaview Books, 1981.

Baseball and Society

Peterson, Robert. *Only the Ball Was White.* Englewood Cliffs, N. J.: Prentice-Hall, 1970.

Roepke, Sharon. *Diamond Gals: The Story of the All American Girls Professional Baseball League.* Marcellus, Mi: AAGBL Cards, 1986.

Rogosin, Donn. *Invisible Men: Life in Baseball's Negro Leagues.* New York: Atheneum, 1985.

Ruck, Rob. *Sandlot Seasons: Sport in Black Pittsburgh.* Chicago: University of Illinois Press, 1987.

Senzel, Howard. *Baseball and the Cold War: Being a Soliloquy on the Necessity of Baseball in the Life of a Serious Student of Marx and Hegel, from Rochester, New York.* New York: Harcourt Brace, 1977.

Tygiel, Jules. *Baseball's Great Experiment: Jackie Robinson and His Legacy.* New York: Random House, 1983.

Baseball and Culture

Asinof, Eliot. *Eight Men Out: The Black Sox and the 1919 World Series.* New York: Holt Rinehart, 1963.

Boyd, Brendan C., and Harris, Fred C. *The Great American Baseball Card Flipping, Trading and Bubble Gum Book.* Boston: Little, Brown, 1973.

Ferretti, Fred. *The Great American Book of Sidewalk, Stoop, Dirt, Curb, and Alley Games.* New York: Workman, 1975.

Smith, Curt. *Voices of the Game: Baseball Broadcasting, 1921 to the Present.* South Bend, Ind: Diamond Communications, 1987.

City Stories

Bready, James. *The Home Team: A Patriotic Story of Baseball in Baltimore.* Baltimore: James Bready, 1958.

Cauz, Louis. *Baseball's Back in Town: A History of Baseball in Toronto.* Toronto: Controlled Media, 1977.

Golenbock, Peter. *Bums: An Oral History of the Brooklyn Dodgers.* New York: Putnam's, 1984.

Hill, Art. *Don't Let Baseball Die: Baseball in Detroit.* Au Train, Mi: Avery Color Studios, 1978.

Overfield, Joseph. *The 100 Seasons of Buffalo Baseball.* Kenmore, N.Y.: Partners' Press, 1985.

Rice, Damon. *Seasons Past: The Story of Baseball's First Century as Witnessed by Three Generations of an American Family.* New York: Praeger, 1976.

Stein, Fred. *Under Coogan's Bluff: A Fan's Recollection of the New York Giants.* Alexandria, Va: Fred Stein, 1978.

Wheeler, Lonnie, and Baskin, John. *The Cincinnati Game.* Wilmington, Ohio: Orange Frazer Press, 1988.

Reference Works

Ercolano, Patrick. *Fungoes, Floaters and Fork Balls: A Colorful Baseball Dictionary.* Englewood Cliffs, N. J.: Prentice-Hall, 1987.

Marazzi, Rich. *The Rules and Lore of Baseball.* New York: Stein and Day, 1980.

Reichler, Joseph, ed. *The Baseball Encyclopedia*, 7th ed. New York: Macmillan, 1988.

Tanner, Chuck, and Enright, Jim. *The Official Major League Baseball Play Book.* Englewood Cliffs, N.J.: Prentice-Hall, 1974.

Wurman, Richard Saul. *Baseball Access.* Los Angeles: Access Press, 1984.

Individual Players

Creamer, Robert. *Babe: The Legend Comes to Life.* Markham, Ont.: Simon and
Schuster, 1974.

Oh, Sadaharu, and Falkner, David. *Sadaharu Oh: A Zen Way of Baseball.*
New York: Times Books, 1984.

Seidel, Michael. *Streak: Joe DiMaggio and the Summer of '41.* New York:
McGraw Hill, 1988.

Ballparks

Lowry, Philip. *Green Cathedrals.* Cooperstown, N.Y.: SABR, 1986.

Shannon, Bill, and Kalinsky, George. *The Ballparks.* New York: Hawthorn,
1975.

Statistical Analysis

James, Bill. *The Bill James Historical Baseball Abstract.* New York: Villard
Books, 1988.

Nemec, David. *Great Baseball Feats, Facts and Firsts.* Scarborough, Ont.:
New American Library, 1987.

Thorn, John, and Holway, John. *The Pitcher.* New York: Prentice-Hall, 1987.

Thorn, John, and Palmer, Pete. *The Hidden Game of Baseball: A Revolutionary
Approach to Baseball and Statistics.* Garden City, N. Y.: Doubleday, 1985.

Baseball Fiction

Craig, John. *Chappie and Me.* New York: Dodd, Mead, 1979.

Holtzman, Jerome, ed. *Fielder's Choice: An Anthology of Baseball Fiction.* New
York: Harcourt Brace, 1979.

Kinsella, W. P. *Shoeless Joe.* Boston: Houghton Mifflin, 1982.

Ongoing Sources

This list of regular sources of information on baseball is deliberately
incomplete and reflects my interests. Two nineteenth-century
publications—*The New York Clipper* and *The Sporting Life*—are now
available only in microfilm but still provide a fresh perspective on the
early days of the game. The Society of American Baseball Research is the
ultimate source for both new and respected annual journals and attending
its yearly convention is a delightful experience.

Roger Angell on baseball: articles appear in *The New Yorker* at mid-season
and there is an end-of-season wrap-up

North American Society for Sport History: *Journal of Sport History* is
published three times a year

Saskatchewan Baseball Hall of Fame: *Saskatchewan Historical Baseball
Review* is published annually

Society for American Baseball Research: publishes *The Baseball Research
Journal, The National Pastime: A Review of Baseball History,* and *The SABR
Review of Books: A Forum of Baseball Literary Opinion*

Sports Illustrated, 1954 to the present

PHOTO CREDITS

INDEX